ODYS ☑ P9-APO-720

Black Pioneers

of Science and Invention

L O U I S   H A B E R

An Odyssey Book
Harcourt Brace & Company
San Diego   New York   London

Requests for permission to make copies of any part of the work
should be mailed to Permissions Department,
Harcourt Brace & Company, 6277 Sea Harbor Drive,
Orlando, Florida 32887-6777.

Library of Congress Cataloging-in-Publication Data
Haber, Louis.
Black pioneers of science and invention/Louis Haber.
p.   cm.
"An Odyssey Book."
Includes bibliographical references and index.
Summary: Traces the lives of black scientists and inventors who have
made significant contributions in the various fields of science and industry.
ISBN 0-15-208566-1 pb
1. Afro-American scientists—Biography—Juvenile literature.
2. Afro-American inventors—Biography—Juvenile literature.
[1. Scientists. 2. Inventors. 3. Afro-Americans—Biography.]
I. Title.
Q141.H2   1992
509.2'2—dc20   91-8923
[B]

Printed in the United States of America
H G F E

Slight revisions to the text of this book have been made in order to reflect
the deaths of some of the individuals included. Otherwise, the text remains
unaltered from the original 1970 edition.

*To my wife Blanche
And my son Richard*

Contents

PREFACE   xi

INVENTORS

BENJAMIN BANNEKER   1

NORBERT RILLIEUX   20

JAN EARNST MATZELIGER   36

ELIJAH McCOY   51

GRANVILLE T. WOODS   60

LEWIS HOWARD LATIMER   71

GARRETT A. MORGAN   88

SCIENTISTS

GEORGE WASHINGTON CARVER 104

PERCY LAVON JULIAN 122

LLOYD A. HALL 146

ERNEST EVERETT JUST 161

DANIEL HALE WILLIAMS 176

LOUIS TOMPKINS WRIGHT 201

CHARLES RICHARD DREW 219

Bibliography 245

Index 257

Contacts with scientists or their relatives provided valuable first-hand materials, and the author is grateful to Dr. Percy L. Julian, Dr. Lloyd A. Hall, Miss Winifred Latimer Norman (granddaughter of Lewis Latimer), Mrs. Charles Drew (widow of Dr. Charles R. Drew), Mrs. Corinne Wright (widow of Dr. Louis T. Wright), and to Garrett A. Morgan, Jr. (son of Garrett A. Morgan).

Preface

This book deals with significant contributions made by black scientists and inventors who were pioneers in the various fields of science, and the roles they played in the development of scientific progress in the United States.

Science textbooks and other books dealing with science contain little if any material dealing with these contributions. While references are often made to the work of George Washington Carver, information about such outstanding black scientists as Benjamin Banneker, Dr. Charles R. Drew, Dr. Percy L. Julian, Dr. Ernest E. Just, and a host of others has not been available to most science teachers and their students. As a result, in classrooms across the nation, except for a few isolated instances, the contributions of black Americans to science and industry have been almost unknown.

Although this book deals solely with the black

scientist in the United States, reference should be made to the early progress of science in Africa. The ancient peoples living in the interior of Africa did not pass through a bronze age. Metals were abundant there, especially iron, and the Africans discovered the use of iron so early that they passed over the bronze age in going from the stone to the iron age. Authorities in anthropology and archaeology concede that Africans were the first to discover iron, the element most useful to man. They learned how to extract iron from the ore that abounds in the interior of Africa and to refine it in furnaces, and blacksmiths throughout Africa worked the metal into useful tools. Other peoples learned to use iron only much later.

In Africa, the black was a discoverer and inventor in spite of his lack of contact with the so-called progressive parts of Asia and Europe. Scientists now give Africans credit for first discovering iron, developing stringed instruments, domesticating the sheep, goat, and cow, and learning about the planetary system. When the black man was brought to the United States and enslaved, all his wits were needed for attempts to make his lot easier in bondage and to obtain his freedom in the face of many obstacles. Yet even while he was engaged in this urgent effort, he succeeded in making a contribution to American invention.

The vast majority of blacks in 1870 were illiterate because they had not been allowed to go to school. In fact, most of the Southern states during slavery had laws prohibiting anyone from teaching slaves to read and write. It is against this background of educational deprivation that the achievements of the black scientist and inventor can be seen in sharpest perspective.

The author began research into this area many years ago. His objective was to gather resource materials that could then be incorporated into science curricula at elementary and secondary schools as well as at the college level. In 1966 he was given a grant from the U.S. Office of Education to pursue this study. After three more years of research, the materials were incorporated into this book.

The Schomburg Collection of the New York Public Library was an excellent source of information and documentation, and the author is indebted to its cooperative staff. The Library of Congress and the National Archives in Washington, D.C., provided much of the primary source material, as well as the Moorland Collection at Howard University in Washington.

Black Pioneers of
Science and Invention

Benjamin Banneker
1731–1806

At a time when President George Washington and Secretary of State Thomas Jefferson were discouraged and felt that their plans for a new capital of the country were doomed to failure, a black surveyor stepped forward and saved the situation. It was through his remarkable talents that the city of Washington, D.C., was finally laid out and completed. Outstanding astronomer, mathematician, and surveyor—this was Benjamin Banneker of colonial times.

Born on a farm outside Baltimore, Maryland, in 1731, Banneker had a most unusual background. The women of his family were of unusual stock. His mother was a freewoman while his father was a slave. His grandmother, Molly Walsh, a white English-woman, had been a dairymaid in England. The story is that on a cold, gray morning in 1698 a cow kicked over a pail of milk and the frightened dairymaid fell off her stool. Molly was brought into court and ac-

Benjamin Bannaker's
PENNSYLVANIA, DELAWARE, MARY-
LAND, AND VIRGINIA
A L M A N A C,
FOR THE
YEAR of our LORD 1795;
Being the Third after Leap-Year.

BANNAKER.

PHILADELPHIA:
Printed for WILLIAM GIBBONS, Cherry Street

Front page of Benjamin Banneker's almanac

cused of stealing the milk. The court did not believe her account of what happened and she was convicted. She was sentenced to serve seven years of bondage in the faraway colony of Maryland.

When Molly had served out her sentence in Maryland and secured her freedom, the first thing she did was to go west and stake out some land for a farm. In those days it was possible to acquire land in that way, although it was extraordinary for a woman to do so, especially by herself. But then Molly Walsh was no ordinary woman! After obtaining the land, she went back to the coast and purchased two male Africans from a slave ship. She married one of the slaves, who was to become Benjamin's grandfather.

Molly and her husband worked on their farm and by dint of great effort and wise planning made it very successful and productive. They raised mainly tobacco and used their product to buy more land. Her husband, Bannaky (later changed to Banneker), was of royal African blood, and he brought with him much of the African culture and agricultural knowledge. This included the art of irrigation, and when neighboring farms suffered from lack of rain, losing their crops as a result, the Banneker farm flourished and prospered. Young Banneker would watch as his grandfather diverted a nearby stream, by means of cleverly built canals, onto the regular rows of tobacco plants. Their farm was the envy of the neighbors.

In time a child was born, a girl, who was named Mary. By the act of 1681, children born of white servant women and Negroes were free. Mary, daughter of Bannaky and Molly Walsh, was a free mulatto. When the time came for Mary to marry, she did the same as her mother had done. She purchased a slave and married him. The product of this marriage was Benjamin Banneker. Being born of a free mother, Benjamin was also free.

When Banneker was twelve years old, a Quaker by the name of Peter Heinrich moved into the valley next to the Banneker farm. Heinrich was to have a profound effect on the young lad, who eventually took over many of the customs and thinking of Quakers, even in dress. When Heinrich opened a school for "all" boys, young Banneker was allowed to enroll, despite the raised eyebrows of many in the white community. He was the only black student in the school. He showed particular interest and a tremendous ability in mathematics and soon progressed beyond the ability of his teacher.

As Banneker grew up, he diligently performed his chores on the farm while his interest in mathematics deepened. He would make up mathematical problems and then solve them. One day, on a trip to the coast to sell the farm's tobacco crop, he met a fascinating man by the name of Josef Levi. Levi showed him a pocket watch, something Banneker had never seen or heard of. Levi explained how it worked and when he saw how excited Banneker became he gave him the watch. Needless to say, Banneker took the watch home and spent days taking it apart and putting it together again until he became thoroughly familiar with the way it worked. Why not make one himself? Off he went to his old teacher, Heinrich, for advice and help. Heinrich wasn't much help but he did give Banneker some material to guide him: an old journal from London that had a picture of a clock, a book on geometry, and Isaac Newton's *Principia* (laws of motion). Armed with these materials, Banneker proceeded to draw plans for a clock, using compass and ruler for measurements, with the picture and the watch as models. He also made the mathematical calculations necessary to make the parts.

For two years Banneker spent all his spare time working on the clock. He built it entirely of wood and carved each of the gears by hand. By 1753 it was completed. It was the first clock ever built in the United States. The clock kept perfect time, striking every hour for more than forty years. People came from all over the country to see his clock. It created a sensation.

When he was twenty-eight years old, Banneker came as close to marriage as he would ever come. He fell in love with Anola, a pretty slave on a nearby plantation. When Anola's master refused to sell her to Banneker, Banneker planned to steal her away and actually booked passage for the two of them on a boat going to England. The plan failed, however, and Banneker was nearly killed in the process. Brokenhearted, Anola committed suicide by drowning. Faithful to her memory, Banneker never married.

In 1772 Andrew Ellicott and his three sons came to the area to build a mill. Banneker and the Ellicotts were to become lifelong friends, working with each other to mutual advantage. This tobacco country seemed a strange place for a mill, but Ellicott felt that tobacco was spoiling the land, taking too much out of the soil. He got the farmers to grow wheat instead. Banneker, forty-one years old at that time, helped the Ellicotts with his knowledge of mechanics, and put together the machinery for the mill. By 1774, two years later, a small village called "Ellicott's Mill" had been laid out. With the coming of the Revolutionary War, wheat became very important as a source of food.

When the Third Continental Congress met in Philadelphia in 1776, Banneker traveled there by horse. There Thomas Jefferson submitted his Declaration of Independence, which stated in part "that all men are created equal; that they are endowed by their Creator with certain unalienable rights; that among these are life, liberty, and the pursuit of happiness." Later Banneker was to remind Jefferson of these wonderful words.

With the Declaration of Independence, the war began. Banneker was so imbued with the spirit he found in Philadelphia that he returned home and planted wheat to feed the Revolutionary Army. He did much to raise food in that whole area for Washington's men, who needed it badly.

During the war, Andrew Ellicott died and left Banneker some books on astronomy and some scientific instruments, including a telescope. Banneker began to study astronomy in earnest and undertook mathematical calculations relating to the stars and the constellations. Based upon his calculations, he predicted that a solar eclipse would take place on April 14, 1789. This was in contradiction to the predictions of two eminent mathematicians and leading astronomers of that time—Leadbetter and Ferguson. Banneker showed where these men had made errors in their calculations, and the eclipse took place just as he had predicted.

Because of his great interest in astronomy and mathematics, Banneker prepared an almanac in 1792 and another each year thereafter for ten years. It included the times of eclipses, the hours of sunrise and sunset, weather forecasts for the year, a tide table for Chesapeake Bay, festival days, holidays, phases of the moon, and so on. His almanac was widely read in the Middle States in the 1790s and was circulated in Pennsylvania, Delaware, Maryland, and Virginia. It became a household staple in early America along with the Bible. Unlike Benjamin Franklin's almanac, for which much of the work was not done by Franklin, all the calculations in Banneker's almanac were made by Banneker himself. He even included a list of medicines to help ward off diseases.

Banneker was deeply concerned over the plight of the Negro slaves and printed a good deal of antislavery material in his almanacs and elsewhere. When he sent a handwritten copy of his first almanac to Thomas Jefferson, then Secretary of State under Washington, he took the opportunity to accompany the almanac with a twelve-page letter in which he defended the mental capacities of the Negro and challenged Jefferson's integrity in the treatment of blacks. Jefferson, a slaveholder himself, had written earlier that "the blacks are inferior to the whites in the endowments both of body and mind." Here, in part, is what Banneker wrote to Jefferson:

> . . . one universal Father hath given being to us all; and he hath not only made us all of one flesh, but he hath also, without partiality, afforded us all the same sensations and endowed us all with the same faculties; and that however variable we may be in society or religion, however diversified in situation or color, we are all in the same family and stand in the same relation to Him.

> . . . it is the indispensable duty of those who maintain for themselves the rights of human nature and who possess the obligations of Christianity, to extend their power and influence to the relief of every part of the human race, from whatever burden or oppression they may unjustly labor under.

> I freely and cheerfully acknowledge that I am of the African race and in that color which is natural to them of the deepest dye; and it is under a sense of the most profound gratitude to

the Supreme Ruler of the Universe that I now confess to you that I am not under that state of tyrannical thraldom and inhuman captivity to which too many of my brethren are doomed, but that I have abundantly tasted of the fruition of those blessings which proceed from that free and unequalled liberty with which you are favored; and which, I hope, you will willingly allow you have mercifully received from the immediate hand of that Being from whom proceedeth every good and perfect Gift.

Suffer me to recall to your mind that time in which the arms and tyranny of the British Crown were exerted with every powerful effort in order to reduce you to a state of servitude.

This, Sir, was a time when you clearly saw into the injustice of a state of slavery and in which you had just apprehensions of the horrors of its condition. It was now that your abhorrence thereof was so excited that you publicly held forth this true and invaluable doctrine which is worthy to be recorded and remembered in all succeeding ages: "We hold these truths to be self-evident, that all men are created equal; that they are endowed by their Creator with certain unalienable rights, and that among these are life, liberty and the pursuit of happiness."

Sir, how pitiable it is to reflect that although you were so fully convinced of the benevolence of the Father of Mankind and of his equal and impartial distribution of these rights and privileges which he hath conferred upon them, that you should at the same time counteract his mercies in detaining by fraud and violence so numerous a part of my brethren under groaning captivity and cruel oppression, that you should at the same time be found guilty of that most criminal act which you professedly detested in others with respect to yourselves.

This was a bold, courageous, and challenging letter. In it, Banneker accused Jefferson of guilt as a slaveholder and of having double standards when he wrote "all men are created equal" and that they are entitled to "life, liberty and the pursuit of happiness." These fine words, said Banneker, should apply to *all* men—black as well as white.

A reply from Jefferson came eleven days later:

I thank you sincerely for your letter of the 19th instant. Nobody wishes more than I do to see such proofs as you exhibit, that nature has given to our black brethren talents equal to those of the other colors of men; and that the appearance of the want of them is owing merely to the degraded condition of their existence both in Africa and America. I can add with truth that nobody wishes more ardently to see a good system commenced for raising the condition, both of their body and mind, to what it ought to be, as far as the imbecility of their present existence and other circumstances, which cannot be neglected, will admit.

I have taken the liberty of sending your Almanac to Monsieur de Condorcet, Secretary of the Academy of Sciences at Paris because I considered it as a document to which your whole color has a right for their justification, against the doubts which have been entertained of them.

I am with great esteem, Sir,

your most obedient, humble servant,

Thomas Jefferson

Philadelphia, August 30, 1791

These letters were part of a long correspondence between Jefferson and Banneker concerning the mental capacities of the Negro and the whole question of slavery.

Banneker's almanacs became almost as famous as his clock. In *A Tribute for the Negro*, published in Manchester, England, Armistead Wilson said of

Sir

Philadelphia Aug. 30. 1791.

I thank you sincerely for your letter of the 19th. instant and for the almanac it contained. no body wishes more than I do to see such proofs as you exhibit, that nature has given to our black brethren, talents equal to those of the other colours of men, & that the appearance of a want of them is owing merely to the degraded condition of their existence both in Africa & America. I can add with truth that no body wishes more ardently to see a good system commenced for raising the condition both of their body & mind to what it ought to be, as fast as the imbecillity of their present existence, and other circumstance which cannot be neglected, will admit. I have taken the liberty of sending your almanac to Monsieur de Condorcet, Secretary of the Academy of sciences at Paris, and member of the Philanthropic society because I considered it as a document to which your whole colour had a right for their justification against the doubts which have been entertained of them. I am with great esteem, Sir

Your most obedt. humble servt.

Th. Jefferson

Mr. Benjamin Banneker
near Elliot's, lower mills. Baltimore county

Letter to Benjamin Banneker from Thomas Jefferson, August 30, 1791 the almanac, "These calculations were so thorough and exact as to excite the approbation of Pitt, Fox, and Wilberforce. One of his almanacs was produced in the British House of Commons as an argument in favor of the mental cultivation of coloured people."

In a preface to Banneker's *Almanack and Ephemeris* of 1796 (the fifth almanac to be issued), the white editor said, "To whom do you think you are indebted for this entertainment? Why, to a Black Man—Strange! Is a Black capable of compiling an almanac? Indeed, it is no less strange than true; and a clever, wise, long-headed Black he is. The labours of the justly celebrated Banneker will likewise furnish you with a very important lesson, Courteous Reader, which you will not find in any other almanac, namely, that the Maker of the Universe is no respector of colours; that the colour of the skin is no way connected with the strength of mind or intellectual powers; that although the God of Nature has marked the face of the African with a darker hue than his brethren, He has given him a soul equally capable of refinement."

In a letter dated August 20, 1791, James McHenry, a prominent Marylander who later served as Secretary of War in Washington's cabinet, made the following references to Banneker: "I consider this Negro as fresh proof that the powers of the mind are disconnected with the colour of the skin, or, in other words, a striking contradiction of Mr. Hume's doctrine that 'the Negroes are naturally inferior to the whites and unsusceptible of attainments in arts and sciences.' "

At about the time that Banneker began working on his almanac, President Washington had decided to move the capital of the country from Philadelphia to a new location that was to be called Washington. He appointed Major Pierre Charles L'Enfant, a young Frenchman who had served with the Continental Army in the Corps of Engineers, to be in charge of building the new city. Major Andrew Ellicott, one of the Ellicott boys, was named Chief Surveyor. At Jefferson's request, Banneker was appointed as the third member of this team.

The assignment was to define the boundaries of the new city and then design and lay out its streets and major buildings. Banneker worked closely with L'Enfant and his maps. But the bureaucrats of that day did not take kindly to a foreigner being given so much power and authority and they interfered in many frustrating ways. This resulted in the highly sensitive and hot-tempered L'Enfant resigning his position and returning to France, taking all the plans and maps with him. Everybody was dismayed and

Jefferson called a meeting of the men involved. What was to be done? Start all over again after more than a year's work? Despair and frustration showed on their faces. Suddenly Banneker asked, "Did you like the plans that were made?" All eyes turned to him. "Of course, but we don't have them." "I think I can reproduce them from memory," said Banneker. The men were astounded and somewhat skeptical. Banneker then went home and, because of his remarkable memory, was able to reproduce all the plans in two days. The work of laying out the city of Washington, with its streets and major buildings, was completed and stands today as a monument to Banneker's genius.

Besides speaking out boldly against the institution of slavery, Banneker was strongly opposed to war. In his almanac for 1792, he proposed the establishment of a Department of Peace within the executive branch of the government with a Secretary of Peace instead of a Secretary of War. His plan included a proposal for free schools for all children and the abolition of capital punishment.

Plan of a Peace-Officer for the United States

Among the many defects which have been pointed out in the federal constitution, it is much to be lamented that no person has taken notice of its total silence upon the subject of an office of the utmost importance to the welfare of the United States, that is, an office for promoting and preserving perpetual peace in our country.

The plan presented seven proposals:

1. Let a Secretary of Peace be appointed to preside in this office.
2. Let a power be given to this Secretary to establish and maintain free schools in every city, village and township of the United States and let him be made responsible for the talents, principles and morals of all his schoolmasters.
3. Let every family in the United States be furnished at the public expense, by the Secretary of this office, with a copy of an American edition of the Bible.
4. Let the following sentence be inscribed in letters of gold over the door of every home in the United States: "The Son Of Man Came Into The World, Not To Destroy Men's Lives But To Save Them."
5. To inspire a veneration for human life and an horror at the shedding of human blood,

let all those laws be repealed which authorize juries, judges, sheriffs, or hangmen to assume the resentments of individuals and to committ murder in cold blood in any case whatever.

6. To subdue that passion for war which education, added to human depravity, has made universal, a familiarity with the instruments of death as well as all military shows should be carefully avoided; military dress and military titles laid aside.

7. Let a large room, adjoining the Federal Hall, be appointed for transacting the business and preserving all the records of this office. Over the door of this room, let there be a sign, on which the figures of a Lamb, a Dove, and an Olive Branch should be painted, together with the following inscription in letters of gold: PEACE ON EARTH—GOOD WILL TO MAN. AH! WHY WILL MEN FORGET THAT THEY ARE BRETHREN?

Banneker spent the later years of his life in retirement on his farm, where he entertained many distinguished men of science and art. They came from all over the world to meet this remarkable scientist, astronomer, mathematician, clock-maker, and surveyor.

On October 25, 1806, Banneker died. The *Federal Gazette and Baltimore Daily Advertiser* of October 28, 1806, carried a notice saying, "known in this neighborhood for his quiet and peaceful demeanor and, among scientists, as an astronomer and mathematician." In his will, Banneker left a number of scientific instruments and many books, as well as a large volume of his manuscripts, to one of the Ellicott boys, George Ellicott. The volume included Banneker's observations on various subjects and copies of all his almanacs, as well as copies of his letters to Thomas Jefferson. All of this is now on display at the Maryland Historical Society.

In France, the Marquis de Condorcet lauded him before the Academy of Sciences. In England, William Pitt placed his name in the records of the Parliament. To the writer's knowledge, no memorial or tablet was erected in this country, nor official recognition given to Banneker's tremendous contributions.

Norbert Rillieux
1806–1894

Very few inventions can be said to be of worldwide significance. It is generally recognized, however, that Norbert Rillieux's invention of the vacuum pan evaporator revolutionized the world's sugar industry. The familiar white, refined crystals of sugar that we take for granted today were made possible by this black man's genius. What is the story of this remarkable inventor?

On March 17, 1806, a child was born on a New Orleans plantation. The child's father was the master of the plantation, a wealthy Frenchman and engineer. His mother was a slave on the plantation. That child was Norbert Rillieux. His birth record, now on file in the city of New Orleans, lists "Norbert Rillieux, quadroon libre, natural son of Vincent Rillieux and Constance Vivant, born March 17, 1806. Baptized in St. Louis Cathedral by Père Antoine."

In his work as an engineer, Rillieux's father was

the inventor of a steam-operated cotton-baling press. Young Norbert's extraordinary ability became apparent at an early age and his father sent him to Paris to be educated. This, no doubt, was dictated by the lack of opportunity for a proper education for him in New Orleans, where educational opportunities for Negroes, free or slave, were unknown. It should be pointed out here that young Rillieux's experience was unlike that of other blacks of his time. He was a free man and was always in a well-to-do and cultured environment because of his father's position and wealth.

In Paris, Norbert turned out to be a brilliant student at L'École Centrale. He showed an extraordinary aptitude for engineering and at the age of twenty-four became an instructor of applied mechanics at L'École Centrale. In 1830 he published a series of papers on steam engine work and steam economy that created favorable attention in scientific circles all over Europe. He also developed the theory of multiple-effect evaporation that was to be the basis for his precedent-shattering invention.

Perhaps Rillieux's interest in the sugar refining process stemmed from his memory of seeing gangs of sweating slaves in New Orleans painfully pouring and ladling boiling sugarcane juice from one steaming, open kettle to another. Until 1846, the trans-

The modern sugar refining industry is based on Norbert Rillieux's
invention of the evaporating pan.

formation of sugarcane juice into sugar was accomplished by this primitive method known as the "Jamaica Train"—a slow and costly process. Although man had finally learned to make sugar from the juice of sugarcane and later from beets, the only sugar available from the "Jamaica Train" process was in dark, crude form, sometimes so crude as to look like molasses. What was needed was some way to refine and granulate sugar so as to produce it with the same sweetness but without the crude effects. This was the task that Rillieux set out to accomplish.

Sugar is easily affected by heat and is caramelized (turned brown) by high heat. Scientists know that by reducing the pressure, the temperature at which a liquid boils can be lowered. This is usually accomplished by boiling the liquid under reduced pressure in a partial vacuum. (A vacuum is an area from which all air has been removed. In a partial vacuum only some of the air is removed.) This process can be applied to liquid sugarcane juice; that is, it can be boiled under a partial vacuum, thus keeping the boiling temperature below the point at which caramelization will take place, and yet boiling and consequent evaporation will be effected.

Before Rillieux, two scientists—Howard and DeGrand—had developed vacuum pans and con-

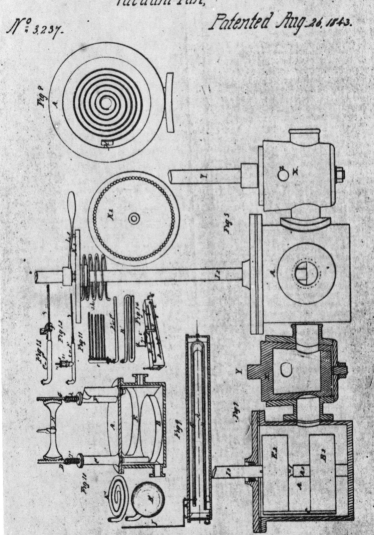

Norbert Rillieux's vacuum pan

densing coils which imperfectly utilized heat in evaporating the liquid portion of the sugarcane juice. It remained for Rillieux, by a stroke of genius, to enclose the condensing coils in a vacuum chamber and to employ the vapor from the first condensing chamber for evaporating the juice in a second chamber under a higher vacuum. The higher the vacuum, the lower the temperature required to evaporate the liquid. The principles involved in this plan laid the foundation for all modern industrial evaporation.

Rillieux's basic inventions are covered by two patents from the United States Patent Office: Patent number 3,237, dated August 26, 1843, and Patent number 4,879, dated December 10, 1846. In the earlier patent, Rillieux describes his invention, in part, in the following words:

The first improvement is in the manner of connecting a steam engine with the evaporating pan or pans in such manner that the engine will be operated by the steam in its passage to the evaporating pan or pans, and the flow of steam be so regulated by a weighted or other valve as to reach the said pan or pans at the temperature required for the process—that is to say, where the saccharine juice boiled—the steam at the same time having access to the pan or evaporator without passing through the engine by the said valve, which is weighted or otherwise regulated to insure the supply of steam to the said pan or evaporator at the required pressure.

In the later patent (1846), after a full description accompanied by complete and elaborate diagrams of his evaporating pans, Rillieux states:

Having thus pointed out the principle or character of my improvements and the manner of constructing and applying the same, what I claim as my invention, and desire to secure by Letters Patent, is—

1. The method of heating the saccharine juice in a heater preparatory to its introduction in the evaporating pans, by means of the waste hot water or escape steam from the evaporating pans.

2. The method of clarifying saccharine juice by heating it in a heater provided with a spout for the discharge of the impurities in the form of scum, and a pipe for drawing off the clear liquid.

3. The method of cooling and partially evaporating saccharine juice or other liquids by discharging the same in the form of spray or

drops in a chamber, where it meets with a current of air; . . . and this I also claim in combination with a condenser whereby the liquid intended to be concentrated is prepared for the evaporating pans and used as a means of condensing the vapor from the pans in which it is to be concentrated or by means of which the water used for the condensing jet is recooled.

4. The method, substantially as described, of combining a vacuum striking pan with a series of evaporating pans, the last of which is independent of the striking pan, and the last of the series of evaporating pans can be in connection with the condenser and work independently of each other.

Evaporation in multiple effect is now universally used throughout the sugar industry as well as in other industries where the evaporation of liquids is an essential process. In the Rillieux evaporator, a series of vacuum pans are so combined as to make use of the heat of the vapor of the evaporation of the juice in the first pan to heat the juice in the second pan, and the vapor heat from the second pan to heat the juice in the third, and so on; the degree of pressure in each successive pan being less. Since the pressure in succeeding pans is less, the liquid boils at a lower temperature, as previously explained. The number of syrup pans may be increased or decreased as needed so long as the last of the series is in conjunction with the condenser, and there is a sufficient temperature difference between the vapor and the liquid to be boiled. The fuel savings made by the use of this latent heat of the vapors are enormous.

News of Rillieux's remarkable work reached the United States and he was offered the post of Chief Engineer in Edmund Forstall's New Orleans sugar factory. He accepted the post, left Paris, and returned to Louisiana. It turned out, however, that Rillieux's father had some disagreement with Forstall, and to avoid displeasing his father, Rillieux gave up the post.

But Rillieux did not remain idle. He designed an evaporator based upon his invention and in 1834 installed the first working model of his triple-effect evaporator on the plantation of Zenon Ramon in Louisiana. Unfortunately there were mechanical difficulties and the machine failed. Another attempt was made in 1841 but it too failed. Rillieux was discouraged and even began to doubt the worth of his invention. Fortunately, however, in 1843 he was induced to try again by Theodore Packwood, the owner of a plantation near New Orleans known as "Myrtle Grove." It took Rillieux two years to design and install the triple-effect evaporator on this plantation. In 1845 the evaporator was put into operation and proved to be a complete success. Packwood received top prizes for the type and quality of the sugar the machine produced.

Public acclaim was widespread. Rillieux had indeed revolutionized the sugar industry. A superior sugar product was secured at a greatly reduced cost. His evaporator did not merely replace a manual operation with a mechanical one; it represented a complete change in theory as well as in method. Where slaves formerly transferred the boiling sugar-cane juice from one boiling kettle to another by means of long ladles, now a single worker operated the completely enclosed machine through outside valves. Besides steam economy and the savings in labor, the loss of sugar was sharply reduced and the quality of the sugar product was considerably raised.

Soon factories all over Louisiana were installing the "Rillieux System." Cuba and Mexico followed soon after. Today the process of evaporation in multiple effects is used universally throughout the sugar industry as well as in the manufacture of condensed milk, soap, gelatin, and glue, and in the recovery of waste liquors in distilleries and paper factories.

The underlying principle on which these evaporators operate has not changed materially since Rillieux first designed his system.

Rillieux himself is described as a man of imposing figure, with "a high forehead, luxuriant white hair and a mustache and full beard trimmed in the French style." On occasion he could be brutally frank. He said exactly what he thought and he could never tolerate dishonesty or injustice. While he became one of the most important men in Louisiana because of his inventions, he was excluded from the social life of his environment. Although not a slave, he was still of the colored race and as such was not socially accepted at the home of any white person. With the approach of the Civil War, free persons of color were more and more restricted. While they had to pay the same taxes as white people, they could not send their children to be educated in the New Orleans public schools. They could not go through the streets of New Orleans without permission. Failure to leave the city when ordered meant years of imprisonment at hard labor. All this Rillieux tolerated with poor grace until he was required by Louisiana to carry a pass. This was too much for him to endure and in 1854 he decided to leave Louisiana forever.

In New Orleans Rillieux had also suffered

professional prejudice when he tried to turn his engineering skills to solving a health problem in that city. New Orleans experienced periodic epidemics of yellow fever during which many of its citizens died. Rillieux knew that yellow fever was carried from person to person by a certain type of mosquito. That mosquito was breeding in the swamps and lowlands of New Orleans. He also knew that mosquitoes breed only in water and therefore could be eliminated by depriving them of water. Rillieux worked out an engineering plan for draining the swamps that would eliminate the places where these mosquitoes were breeding. With the mosquitoes gone, yellow fever would be wiped out. He submitted this plan to the city sewerage system. The plan was turned down because it was the work of a black man! Years later, after Rillieux was gone, the city was forced to put an essentially similar plan into operation.

So in 1854 we find Rillieux back in Paris. He seems to have given up his profession and for the next ten years occupied himself with the study of Egyptology and the deciphering of hieroglyphics. In his later years, however, he turned again to engineering and invention. France at that time was producing most of its sugar from sugar beets. Rillieux applied his evaporating-pan process to sugar beets, and in 1881, at the age of seventy-five, patented a process of heating juices with vapors in multiple effect which is still used in cane and beet sugar factories throughout the world. Production costs, in terms of reduced fuel consumption, were cut in half and a better sugar product resulted.

In his eighties, Rillieux's health began to fail. He died on October 8, 1894, at the age of eighty-nine, and was buried in a vault in the Père Lachaise Cemetery in Paris. Today, this inscription can be seen over his grave:

Ici reposent
Norbert Rillieux
Ingénieur civil à la Nouvelle-Orléans
18 Mars 1806
Décéde à Paris le 8 Octobre 1894
Emily Cuckow, Veuve Rillieux
1827–1912

This inscription gives the first inkling that Rillieux had a wife. The author has been unable to find any material relating to Mrs. Rillieux other than the simple inscription giving her name and dates of birth and death. She was apparently twenty-one years younger than Rillieux and died eighteen years after his death.

While in his day Rillieux was recognized and widely acclaimed for his precedent-making inventions in the sugar industry, he is virtually unknown today. His name does not appear in chemistry or physics textbooks or in technical journals. Yet in 1903, J. G. McIntosh, in his book *Technology of Sugar*, published in London, devoted five pages to the development, principle, and advantages of Rillieux's patents. He wrote, "This is the system which constitutes the basis of all the saving in fuel hitherto effected in sugar factories. Rillieux may therefore, with all justice, be regarded as one of the greatest benefactors of the sugar industry."

Charles A. Browne, an outstanding sugar chemist of the United States Department of Agriculture, stated, "I have always held that Rillieux's invention is the greatest in the history of American chemical engineering and I know of no other invention that has brought so great a saving to all branches of chemical engineering." Alfred Webre, a specialist in the field of evaporation, felt that Rillieux was fifty to seventy-five years ahead of his time with many of his ideas.

Rillieux is also credited with many engineering devices now in use, such as the "catchall" for preventing the carrying over of sugar from one pan to another by droplets in the vapor; the sight glass or "lunette" for watching the progress of the evaporation in the vacuum apparatus; and the substitution of cast-iron vessels for the costly copper vessels which were previously thought to be essential for sugar evaporation.

More than thirty years after Rillieux's death, a worldwide movement was initiated to give honor and recognition to him for his highly significant contributions to the sugar industry. The movement began in Holland and quickly spread to include organizations representing every sugar-producing country in the world. A bronze plaque was designed in Amsterdam which was subsequently placed in the Louisiana State Museum in New Orleans, where it now stands. The plaque shows a bust of the inventor and bears the heading "Norbert Rillieux, 1806–1894." In a frame of tiles, also made in Holland, the following inscription appears:[1]

To honor and commemorate
Norbert Rillieux
born at New Orleans, La., March 18, 1806
and died at Paris, France, October 8, 1894

[1] The date of his birth on his grave and on this tablet does not correspond to Rillieux's birth record in New Orleans. The use of the word "corporations" in the inscription is somewhat misleading, as the contributors were scientific and technological organizations and not commercial corporations.

Inventor of Multiple Evaporation and its
Application into the Sugar Industry
This tablet was dedicated in 1934 by
Corporations representing the Sugar
Industry all over the world

Jan Earnst Matzeliger
1852–1889

The modern shoe industry in this country and in the world is based upon a revolutionizing invention patented by a young black genius in 1883. What Eli Whitney's invention of the cotton gin did for the South, what Elias Howe's invention of the sewing machine did for the garment industry, what Rillieux's invention of the vacuum-pan evaporator did for the sugar industry, that is what Matzeliger's invention of the shoe-lasting machine did for the shoe industry. How did it happen?

Jan Matzeliger was born in Paramaribo, Surinam (Dutch Guiana), on September 15, 1852. His mother was a native Negro of Surinam. His father was a Dutch engineer who had been sent to Paramaribo, a colony of Holland at that time, to take charge of the government machine works. He is described as an educated man and a member of a very wealthy and aristocratic family in Holland.

Jan E. Matzeliger revolutionized the shoe industry.

At the age of ten, young Matzeliger was put to work as an apprentice in the government machine shops. There he showed a remarkable talent for mechanics, which, no doubt, served him well in his work on the shoe-lasting machine some twenty years later.

Not happy with life in Dutch Guiana, Jan decided to seek his fortune elsewhere. At the age of nineteen he shipped out as a sailor on an East Indian merchant ship, not knowing exactly what he wanted to do. He worked on the ship for two years. By that time he had had enough of the sea and wanted to try his hand at some work more closely related to his former training in mechanics. He left the ship in Philadelphia and spent a year or two there working at odd jobs, including an apprenticeship as a cobbler of shoes.

By 1876 Matzeliger had tired of Philadelphia, or perhaps opportunities for blacks there were not too fruitful. In any event, he went to Boston and worked there for a year before moving on to Lynn, Massachusetts, where he was to remain for the rest of his life. It was in Lynn that he met and solved the problem of making shoes completely by machine.

At that time, Lynn was a town of about 35,000 people. It was already the largest shoe manufacturing center in the country in a state that was responsible for more than one-half of the shoes produced in the United States. Because of his knowledge of mechanics and cobbling, he was able to secure a job with Harney Brothers, a shoe manufacturing factory, operating a McKay sole-sewing machine for shoes. Other jobs followed where Matzeliger had an opportunity to work on the different kinds of machines used in making shoes. Soon he became familiar with most of the machines then in use in the shoemaking industry.

When he came to Lynn, young Matzeliger had very little knowledge of the English language; in fact, he had never had any kind of formal education. But after work he would go to evening school, where he made excellent progress. Besides learning English, he bought books on physics and other subjects from his very meager earnings. An industrious individual, he was always working and always studying. Although lonely in a new land, he is described as cheerful, kindhearted, pleasant, of a friendly nature, honest, and modest.

When he tried to join one of the white churches in Lynn, he found that being a Negro was a handicap to becoming a member of the local Catholic, Episcopal, and Unitarian churches. It was not until 1884, five years before his death, that he was welcomed into the Christian Endeavor Society, a youth group of the North Congregational Church. While he never was made an official member of the church, he did attend services and even taught Sunday school there. This church was in later years to remember

Matzeliger with gratitude when it was threatened with financial ruin.

What about Matzeliger's shoe machine? While there were several machines in use in the shoe-making industry, there was no machine for connecting the "uppers" to the soles of the shoe. This had to be done by hand, and it was generally felt in the industry that no machine could ever be devised to do this task. They said it just could not be done! This was a challenge which Matzeliger readily accepted. Although men jeered at him for thinking he could invent such a machine and many a joke was turned at his expense, Matzeliger was not deterred.

What machines were available at that time? It was in 1790 that Thomas Saint, a London cabinet-maker, invented the first sewing machine designed to be used on shoe leather. Twenty years later, Marc Brunel, a French refugee in London, set up machines for mass producing nailed army shoes. It took another thirty-one years (1841) for Thomas Archbold, an English machinist, to apply the principle of the eyepointed needle to shoe production. There were a few machines produced in the United States for mechanically producing certain parts of the shoe but no machine that could *last* shoes; that is, connect the upper part of the shoe to the sole. Several lasting machines had been tried but had failed miserably.

Lasting still had to be done by hand. While the hand lasters were highly skilled workers and were paid well, their work was necessarily slow and production was small. In fact, the hand lasters proved to be "bottlenecks" in the production of shoes, since the other shoe parts, produced by fast machines, would pile up to await finishing by the hand lasters. As a result, shoe production was restricted by the slow pace of hand lasting and the price of shoes was consequently high.

Matzeliger would watch the hand lasters at their work very closely. His machine would have to duplicate the movements of their fingers from stretching the leather into place at the toe and heel to the final tacking operations. Once he had learned their technique, he rented a cheap room over the old West Lynn Mission and there he experimented at night, after putting in long and exhausting hours at his regular job during the day. The lack of proper heating facilities did not improve his health, and in all probability contributed a great deal to his contracting tuberculosis later in life. For his experiments, he utilized pieces of wood, old cigar boxes, and other scrap materials, and he improvised tools. He experimented with one idea after another. Some ideas were good, others proved to be worthless.

After six months of hard work, he had a crude model which worked. He was offered fifty dollars for the model but he refused the offer. Years went by with constant experimentation and not a little discouragement before Matzeliger succeeded in making a model machine which was capable of pleating the leather around the toe and heel of a shoe. This had never been done by machine and he was offered fifteen hundred dollars for the model, but again he refused. He was not as yet satisfied that he had licked the problem of turning out a complete shoe by machine. The year was 1880.

By this time Matzeliger had gotten permission to do his work in a separate section of a plant where he was able to make use of an old discarded forge for making the various parts of his experimental machine. Not having the money to hire help, he did the grueling work of filing, forging, machining, and fitting all by himself. For years he lived on very little, spending no more than five or six cents a day on food, in order to save his money for his project.

Although very poor and in ill health, he began work on a third machine. This time even his scrimping and saving was not enough. He went out to seek financial support so as to be able to continue his work. He succeeded in getting the financial backing of Melville S. Nichols and Charles H. Delnow in exchange for a two-thirds interest in the invention.

It was three years after the completion of his second machine that Matzeliger finally achieved what he was after—a lasting machine that could turn out a complete shoe. Patent number 274,207 was granted to him on March 20, 1883, by the United States Patent Office. It took seven pages of complicated drawings and eight pages of closely printed descriptive material to describe the lasting machine for the Patent Office. To give the reader some idea of what the machine actually did, here is part of the patent application:

> My invention relates to the lasting of boots and shoes. The object of it is to perform by machinery and in a more expeditious and economical manner the operations which have heretofore been performed by hand. Heretofore devices have been contrived for performing a part of the operation, such as holding the last in proper position and drawing the leather over the last, while the nailing was done by hand. In my machine, I perform all the operations by the machine, and automatically, requiring only the service of a boy or girl or other unskilled labor to attend the

machine. My invention includes the mechanism for holding the last in place and allowing it to be turned and the last fed forward in proper position for the operation of the machine. It includes a feeding device for moving the last step by step at a proper distance, whereby the mechanism for drawing over the leather may operate successively and at proper intervals. It includes pinchers or gripping mechanism for drawing the upper over the last, mechanism for turning the gripping mechanism in order to plait the leather at the heel or toe, mechanism for holding the last in proper position for the operation of the feeding mechanism, mechanism for feeding the nails and holding them in proper position to be driven, and mechanism for driving the nails at the proper instant.

From this description it can be seen that Matzeliger's lasting machine could hold the last in position and move it forward while other parts punched the leather and drew it over the last, fitting the leather at the toe and heel. Nails were fed into position and driven into place, and all this was done so smoothly that a shoe could be completed in the space of one minute! In a factory test, the machine made a record run of lasting seventy-five pairs of women's shoes in one day! Later, the machine was made to turn out 150 to 700 pairs of shoes in one day, depending upon the quality of the work. Compare this production with that of an expert hand laster, who could handle fifty pairs of shoes in a ten-hour day. The shoe industry had indeed been revolutionized! A young Negro genius, without the aid of a formal education, had achieved the impossible.

The new machine not only greatly increased shoe production; it also cut the cost of shoes by half. By 1889 the demand for the new lasting machine became worldwide. Matzeliger continued to work to improve his machine and received four additional patents:

1. Mechanism for distributing tacks and nails.
   Patent number 415,726, October 12, 1888.
2. Nailing machine (improvements in tack and nail distribution and driving mechanism).
   Patent number 421,954, February 25, 1890.
3. Tack separating and distributing mechanism.
   Patent number 423,937, March 25, 1890.
4. Lasting machine.
   Patent number 459,899, September 22, 1891.

J. E. MATZELIGER.
LASTING MACHINE.

No. 274,207.   Patented Mar. 20, 1883.

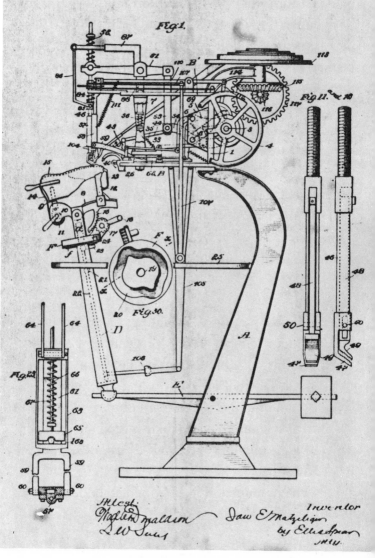

Jan Matzeliger's lasting machine

Matzeliger and his financial backers, Delnow and Nichols, set up the Union Lasting Machine Company, in which Matzeliger owned a block of stock. However, the capital needed to go into large-scale production was too much for this small company. Outside financial help was needed. George W. Brown and Sidney W. Winslow were interested and willing to help. They formed the Consolidated Lasting Machine Company, which took over Matzeliger's patents in exchange for a block of stock. Rapid production of the new machine began in the middle eighties and expanded rapidly. By 1897 Winslow was able to bring together the major lasting-machine manufacturers of the country to organize a holding company, the New York Machine Company. But by this time Matzeliger was out of the picture. In 1899 Winslow completed his consolidation of machine manufacturing companies to form the United Shoe Machinery Corporation with a capitalization of twenty million dollars and with himself as president. During the next twelve years, this corporation earned more than fifty million dollars and had captured 98 percent of the shoe machinery business. By 1955 its capitalization was over a billion dollars.

How many people today connect the multimillion-dollar United Shoe Machinery Corporation with the name of Matzeliger? How ironic it is that his memory is preserved in the name of his machine as it is known in the shoe industry—the "Nigger Head" machine.

What was Matzeliger's reward? Because of his long and hard work, day and night, and lack of proper food and warmth because of his extreme poverty, Matzeliger's health suffered. In the summer of 1886 he contracted a cold which, due to his low resistance, turned into tuberculosis. For three years he was bedridden and he finally succumbed on August 24, 1889, at the age of thirty-seven. He is buried in the Pine Grove Cemetery at Lynn, Massachusetts. How much more this genius could have contributed had he been able to live a normal span of life!

Some years before his death, Matzeliger became a member of a white church in Lynn, the North Congregational Society. As previously stated, he had been rejected by the other churches and he apparently neither forgot nor forgave. In his will, Matzeliger bequeathed to North Church all of his holdings in the Union Lasting Machine Company plus one-third of his interest in the Consolidated Lasting Machine Company with the proviso that the money "shall not knowingly be given or expended for any member of the Roman Catholic, Unitarian, and Episcopal churches."

Years later, the North Congregational Church became heavily involved in debt and remembered the stock that had been left to it by this colored member. They found, upon inquiry, that it had become very valuable through the importance of the patent under the management of the large company then controlling it. The church sold the stock and realized from its sale more than enough to pay off the entire debt of the church, which amounted to $10,860. With the canceled mortgage as the incentive, the church held a special service of thanks one Sunday morning. A life-sized portrait of Matzeliger, their benefactor, looked down from the platform on the immense congregation below, while a young white lady, a member of the church, read a eulogy of the deceased and the pastor, the Reverend A. J. Covell, preached an eloquent sermon, the text found in Romans 13:8, "Owe no man anything but to love one another." The portrait of Matzeliger has become a permanent part of the vestry room of this church.

It is interesting to note that after the Russian Revolution, some Russian engineers came to the

United States to study modern shoe production. They were so impressed with Matzeliger's work and his lasting machine that upon their return to Russia they wrote and published Matzeliger's story in their own language.

Elijah McCoy
1844–1929

The expression "It's the real McCoy" has very much become a part of our everyday vocabulary. But how many of us know how it came to be used—or that it is associated with the pioneering work of a black engineer?

Let us go back to a day in 1844 in Canada, where Elijah McCoy was born. Why in Canada? Because his parents were fugitive slaves who escaped from Kentucky through the "underground railroad"—so called because it was a movement made up of Abolitionists and others who felt very strongly that slavery was an evil institution and who helped move escaped slaves from the South into Canada where they could live as free men and women.

McCoy was born in Colchester, Ontario, in Canada on May 2, 1844. Some time later the family moved back to the United States and settled in a place about one mile west of Ypsilanti, Michigan.

Elijah McCoy, father of lubrication

There young McCoy attended grammar school. It is not known whether he ever finished grammar school before he decided to go to Edinburgh, Scotland, to serve an apprenticeship in mechanical engineering. As a youth, he had always been interested in machinery and things mechanical. He was always "tinkering" with any machines he could lay his hands on and was usually successful in fixing them. He wanted to make engineering his life's work.

After finishing his apprenticeship in Scotland, McCoy returned to the United States a full-fledged mechanical engineer. However, here he encountered race prejudice. Companies employing mechanical engineers at that time were unwilling to hire a black man in such a highly skilled position. He finally secured a job as a fireman on the Michigan Central Railroad, where one of his duties was to oil the engine. In those days, it was customary to stop the trains periodically, when they thought it was time, and the oilman would go around oiling all moving parts of the train—the engine, the wheels, and so on. The same thing was done in factories, where all machinery would be shut down from time to time so that the moving parts could be oiled or lubricated.

Lubrication is essential in machinery because if the moving parts of a machine come into contact with each other, the machine will soon stop. The friction developed between the moving parts would make them so hot that they would stick together or "burn out." Friction is prevented by covering these moving parts with a thin film of oil or grease called a "lubricant." The machine parts meet little resistance as they slide over this slick film, since friction is reduced.

There are three kinds of lubricants: solid, partly solid, and liquid. Solid lubricants are made from minerals such as graphite (a form of carbon). These lubricants are used mostly on wood and rough metal. They create a slippery surface by filling up the cracks.

Partly solid lubricants are made from animal and vegetable oils. They are actually thick greases, and are used chiefly on slow-moving machinery.

Liquid lubricants are the most frequently used of the three kinds. They come from crude oil or petroleum, a complex mixture of hydrocarbons (chemical compounds made up only of the elements hydrogen and carbon). The lubricants are separated from the mixture by a process known as fractional distillation, where the mixture is heated to high temperatures and different chemicals (fractions) in the crude oil are drawn off at different temperatures. Lubricating oils are drawn off at approximately 300°C. These liquid lubricants are used in most machinery having moving parts. They are used in automobiles, where, in winter, light, thin lubricants are used because the cold air would thicken a heavy oil so much that the lubricant itself would offer resistance to the moving parts of the engine. In summer, when the heat causes even heavy oils to become rather thin, heavier oils are used to lubricate the auto-mobile engine.

McCoy became interested in the problems of lubricating machinery. He felt that the periodic and frequent shutting down of machinery for oiling or lubrication was a waste of both time and money— and furthermore was unnecessary. In his crude machine shop, he tried various devices that would lubricate machines as they worked, thereby doing away with the necessity of stopping them at any time. His idea was to provide, in the making of the machine, for certain canals with connecting devices to distribute the oil throughout the machinery and whenever needed, rather than have to figure out the need from memory—in other words, to make lubrication automatic. He called his device the "lubricating cup."

In July, 1872, McCoy patented his first invention of an automatic lubricator, a device that, in his words, "provided for the continuous flow of oil on the gears and other moving parts of a machine in order to keep it lubricated properly and continuously and thereby do away with the necessity of shutting down the machine periodically." This invention was particularly applicable to the steam engine and steam cylinder. It provided for an oil cup built in as part of the steam cylinder. A hollow stem projected down from the bottom of the cup into the steam cylinder. A rod, through this hollow stem, had a valve at the upper end and a piston at the lower end. When the steam in the cylinder pressed upon the piston, the valve rose and allowed the oil in the cup to pass out to lubricate the cylinder automatically.

A year later, McCoy improved on his original invention of a steam cylinder lubricator by providing additional devices so that the lubricator oiled chiefly when the steam was exhausted. This was the time when the oil was most needed. (See page 57). Further improvements were made in later years and these were also patented by McCoy. Factories everywhere were quick to adopt McCoy's lubricating cups.

In 1892, McCoy turned his attention to the problems of lubrication for railroad locomotives and invented a number of devices for lubricating locomotive engines. At one point, the inability to secure equalization of the steam pressure in the locomotive engine prevented the steam from entering the engine, thereby preventing proper lubrication. McCoy overcame this difficulty by the use of an independent steam pipe and an independent overflow pipe. In this way he secured a perfect equalization of the steam pressure going in and out of the engine, resulting in proper lubrication. His system was soon

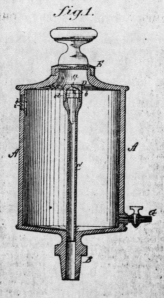

Elijah McCoy's automatic lubricator

in use on all railroads in the West and on steamers on the Great Lakes.

As late as 1920, McCoy applied his lubrication system to the air brakes on locomotives and other vehicles employing air brakes. His inventions in that field related to the means of lubricating the pistons of the steam and air cylinders for the air brakes. His device supplied a mixture of oil and graphite to the steam cylinders, and dry graphite to the air cylinders. This improved the operation of air brakes tremendously.

McCoy held over fifty patents. With the exception of a patent for an "Ironing Table" and one for a "Lawn Sprinkler," all the others were in the field of automatic lubrication. Small wonder, then, that he is so often referred to as "the father of lubrication." He was a pioneer in the art of steadily supplying oil to machinery in intermittent drops from a cup, doing away with the necessity of shutting down the machine to lubricate it. McCoy's lubricating systems ultimately came into general use on industrial and locomotive machinery throughout this country and elsewhere in the world.

Such extensive use was made of his inventions that after a while no piece of heavy-duty machinery was considered complete unless it had the "McCoy system." People inspecting a new piece of machinery would make sure that it had automatic lubrication by asking, "Is it the real McCoy?" Today the expression "It's the real McCoy" is used to indicate perfection.

Granville T. Woods
1856–1910

Known as the "Black Edison" by many in the electrical industry because of his persistent and successful investigations into the mystery of electricity, Granville Woods surpassed most men in this field in the number and variety of his inventions of important and significant electrical systems and devices.

Woods was born in Columbus, Ohio, on April 23, 1856. At ten years of age he had to go to work and never had the chance to complete his elementary school education. At an early age he worked in a machine shop, and it can be said that he learned his skills by "on-the-job" training.

In 1872, at the age of sixteen, Woods moved to Missouri, where he worked both as firemen and engineer on the railroads. There his interest in electricity began and developed. He spent all his leisure time studying electricity, taking books from the pub-

Granville T. Woods, the "Black Edison"

lic library and borrowing books on the subject from friends and sympathetic employers. When he had gotten as much knowledge as he could from these books, he went east to take a course in electrical and mechanical engineering. For the most part, he was self-taught.

With his new training and ability, he got a job as engineer on the *Ironsides*, a British steamer, where he remained for two years. Later on, he secured a position as engineer on the Danville and Southern Railroad which served to stimulate many of the ideas that he later used in his inventions.

By 1881, he had reached a new stage in his development and he settled down in Cincinnati, Ohio. He opened a factory, where he manufactured telephone, telegraph, and electrical equipment. He became interested in thermal power (power through heat) and steam-driven engines, and in 1884 he filed his first patent application for an improved steam-boiler furnace. The patent was granted.

In the same year, Woods invented a telephone transmitter.[1] Essentially, the telephone transmitter is a device for sending sound over a distance by means of the electric current. Sounds are caused by vibrations. In the telephone transmitter, the sound of the voice causes a thin metal disk or diaphragm to vibrate. As the diaphragm vibrates, or bends back and forth, it presses against a little box full of tiny grains of carbon. When these grains are pressed together they conduct the electricity well. When the diaphragm bends the other way, the grains are no

[1] U.S. Patent number 308,817, December 2, 1884.

longer pressed together and the electricity is conducted poorly. This produces a series of strong and weak currents, which is conducted by wires to the telephone receiver at the other end. There it causes an electromagnet to pull a diaphragm weakly or strongly, depending upon the strong and weak currents coming from the transmitter. This sets the diaphragm in the receiver to vibrate in exactly the same way as the diaphragm in the transmitter. These vibrations are then transformed into sound.

The object of Woods' invention was to produce a telephone transmitter with more distinct and powerful effects than had been possible at that time by the type of electrical current then being used. By producing and making use of alternating current, controlled by the action of vibrating diaphragms, he was able to construct a telephone transmitter that could carry the voice over much longer distances than the transmitter then in use, with louder and more distinct sound.

One year after his invention of the telephone transmitter, Woods patented an apparatus that combined the telegraph with the telephone.[2] He coined the word "telegraphony" for it (telegraph plus telephone). By means of his apparatus, one did not have

[2] U.S. Patent number 315,368, April 7, 1885.

to be an experienced telegraph operator to send telegraph messages. If the operator could not read or write the Morse signals, he had only to "cut" the battery out of the main-line circuit by means of a switch, cut it into a local circuit, and then speak near the telegraph key. When this was done, the telegraph sounder at the receiving station would cause the air to vibrate in unison with the electric waves that came over the wire. The person at the receiving station would thus receive the message as articulate speech. In this way, at telegraph stations both oral and signal messages could be transmitted over the same line without any change in the instruments. This did away with the disadvantages of requiring skillful operators of telegraph equipment and the need to know the Morse code. The invention was purchased by the American Bell Telephone Company of Boston, Massachusetts, for a handsome sum of money.

In 1887, Woods' inventive and brilliant mind brought forth one of his most important inventions —railway telegraphy.[3] By means of this invention, messages could be sent between moving trains, and from moving trains to a railroad station and back. It is very important for the conductor or engineer of

[3]U.S. Patent number 373,383, November 15, 1887.

G. T. WOODS.

APPARATUS FOR TRANSMISSION OF MESSAGES BY ELECTRICITY.

No. 315,368.

Patented Apr. 7, 1885.

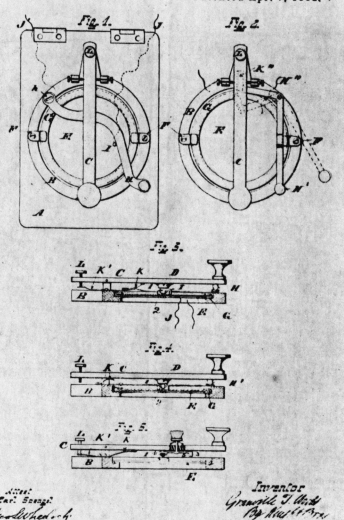

Granville T. Woods' invention of "telegraphony"

a train to be able to send and receive messages while the train is going along its route. Serious accidents can be prevented, and consequent loss of life, if the engineer is forewarned of a washed-out bridge or some obstacle of which he is not aware in the path of the train. Here Woods took advantage of the fact that ordinary lines of telegraph wires usually ran along and parallel to the railroad tracks. His device conducted the messages from the train, by static electricity, to the telegraph wires running beside the track. The messages could then be conducted along these wires to their destination. It in no way interfered with the ordinary use of the telegraph wires.

With this invention, Woods organized his own company, the Woods Electric Company, to take over and exploit his patents. However, the demand for his electrical devices became so widespread that he abandoned his idea of marketing these appliances and instead devoted his whole time to invention. The company was in existence from 1887 to 1893.

In 1890 Woods moved to New York City, where he continued his career. In his work he had the cooperation of his brother, Lyates Woods, who also had a number of appliances of considerable commercial value in his own right.

In New York City, Woods attended the theater

whenever he had the time. He was intrigued by the way in which the theater lights were "dimmed" gradually until they went out completely. He found out that this was accomplished by means of a bulky mechanical resistor which was wired in series with the lights. This type of resistor was also used to control or vary the strength of the electric current in many other pieces of electrical equipment, such as the motor that controlled the operation of an elevator. The trouble with this system was that the resistor would get very hot. This was wasteful in terms of electrical energy being lost in the form of heat—and moreover it was a serious fire hazard. Fires in theaters and elsewhere from these resistors were not uncommon.

Woods set out to produce an economical, efficient, and safe system for controlling and operating such electrical devices. In 1896 he invented a system that would do this by arranging, in the circuit between the generator and the device to be protected, a separate generator that could vary, as desired, the strength of the electrical current delivered to the device.[4] His system was not only safe and efficient, it also brought about a savings in electricity of over 40 percent.

[4]U.S. Patent number 569,443, October 13, 1896.

Woods' ideas and inventions did much to change and modernize transportation. He made it possible to go from inefficient, costly, steam-engine-driven trains to cleaner, cheaper, and more effective train engines run by electricity. In 1888 he set up an overhead conducting system for electric railways. In this system a pole from the train or trolley car drew the electricity needed to run the locomotive's motor from a power line running overhead along the path of the train or trolley. This became a familiar sight in many cities. In fact, it was not long before large cities began to prohibit steam engine trains, with their black clouds of smoke and soot, from entering the city area. Before coming into the city, the train had to switch to an electrically driven engine. Woods also invented what is now referred to as the "third rail," now in use in the subway systems of New York City and elsewhere.[5] He did this by setting up a series of conductors of electricity along and parallel to the path of the train. "Collectors" of this electricity were carried by each car on the train and were adapted so as to connect or make contact with the conductors on the ground along the route. Electricity was controlled by means of electromagnetic switches between the ground conductors and

[5] U.S. Patent number 667,110, January 29, 1901.

the supply or source of electricity. Woods sold this invention to the General Electric Company of New York in 1901.

In the years 1902, 1903, and 1905, Woods invented a series of devices which resulted in the automatic air brake, which he sold to the Westinghouse Air Brake Company of Pennsylvania. Fifteen years later, in 1920, Elijah McCoy was to invent a system of lubrication for these air brakes.

The electrical management of hatching chicken eggs became another of Woods' inventions. In 1890 he came out with an egg incubator heated by electricity. The internal temperature of the incubator was rigidly controlled by means of an electric thermostat, much like the thermostats that are now used in homes to control the heat inside a house.

In addition, Woods' inventions include a Relay Instrument (1887), an electromechanical brake (1887), an electromagnetic brake apparatus (1887), a Tunnel Construction for electric railways (1888), a galvanic battery (1888), an automatic safety cut-out for electric circuits (1889), an amusement apparatus (1889), and many others.

In the field of electric railways alone, Woods was granted fifteen patents, and he held a still larger number of patents on systems and devices for the control and distribution of electricity. He had more than sixty patents to his credit when he died in 1910. Records in the United States Patent Office show assignments of his patents to the General Electric Company in New York, the Westinghouse Air Brake Company in Pennsylvania, the American Bell Telephone Company in Boston, and the American Engineering Company of New York.

Few inventors of any race have produced a larger number of appliances in the field of electricity, and few have done more for the electrical industry than Granville Woods. His work continued without interruption for over a quarter of a century.

Today we owe much to the brilliance and industry of Granville Woods, who, with his contemporary, Lewis Latimer (pages 71–87), gave us much of what we now take for granted in the field of electricity.

Lewis Howard Latimer
1848–1928

A black slave escaped from Virginia and fled to Boston, Massachusetts; not an unusual occurrence in the 1830s. The slave, George Latimer, settled in Boston with his family and lived there for several years. In October, 1842, his owner, James B. Gray, came to Boston to claim Latimer as his property. The Latimer case became the first of several famous Boston fugitive slave cases. Abolitionists such as William Lloyd Garrison and Frederick Douglass took up Latimer's cause. One month later four hundred dollars was raised to purchase Latimer's freedom. Shortly thereafter Massachusetts passed a Personal Liberty Law forbidding state officers from participating in hunting for fugitive slaves. Such was the story of George Latimer, the father of our scientist and inventor, Lewis Howard Latimer.

Lewis was born in Chelsea, Massachusetts, on the fourth day of September, 1848, six years after

Lewis Howard Latimer—Edison Pioneer

his father had secured his freedom. As a young boy,
after school, he was on the streets selling *The Liberator*, a newspaper written by William Lloyd Garrison and devoted to the abolition of slavery.

Lewis's childhood was brief. When he was ten
years old, his father deserted the family, leaving his
mother with four young children. Lewis had to give

up any further ideas about school and went to work to support himself and help support his family. During the Civil War, at the age of sixteen, he enlisted in the United States Naval Service and served as "landsman" on the U.S.S. *Massasoit*. He was a credit to his country, as were his brothers who were fighting with the Union's land forces. Lewis was honorably discharged in 1865 and returned to Boston to seek employment.

Lewis Latimer had a talent for drawing and loved to paint. When Crosby & Gould, patent solicitors, were looking for an office boy with a "bent for drawing," he applied for and got the job. Applications for patents have to be accompanied by detailed drawings to help describe the device to be patented. Because of this, Crosby & Gould hired a number of draftsmen to work on such drawings. It was in this office that Latimer became interested in drafting. With a secondhand set of drafting tools purchased out of his meager earnings, together with some library books on the subject and the aid of some kind draftsmen, Latimer gradually learned enough about drafting to approach his employer and ask that he be permitted to make some drawings. The request was grudgingly granted. As it turned out, his work was so outstanding that he was given a job as draftsman in the office and eventually went on to become the chief draftsman of Crosby & Gould, remaining with the company for about eleven years.

It was during this time that Latimer met and fell in love with Mary Wilson. They were married on December 10, 1873. A gifted amateur poet whose poetry was later published in a volume entitled *Poems of Love and Life*, Latimer wrote the following poem for the occasion:

Ebon Venus

Let others boast of maidens fair,
Of eyes of blue and golden hair;
My heart like needles ever true
Turns to the maid of ebon hue.

I love her form of matchless grace,
The dark brown beauty of her face,
Her lips that speak of love's delight,
Her eyes that gleam as stars at night.

O'er marble Venus let them rage,
Who set the fashions of the age;
Each to his taste, but as for me,
My Venus shall be ebony.

A modern title for this poem could very well be "Black Is Beautiful."

The office where Latimer was employed was located near the school where Alexander Graham Bell taught deaf-mute people. In the course of trying to invent a machine that would enable deaf persons to hear, Bell invented the telephone. He needed a skilled draftsman to assist him with the patent applications and he asked Latimer to work with him. It was Latimer who executed the drawings and assisted in preparing the descriptions required to prepare the applications for the telephone patent of Alexander Graham Bell. The patent was issued in 1876.

Having a creative and inventive mind, and stimulated, no doubt, by working in an office where applications for patents on inventions were being processed, Latimer began to work on inventions of his own. One of his earliest inventions, patented on February 10, 1874,[1] dealt with "Water Closets For Railroad Cars." His invention added a closed, pivoted bottom to the usual open-end water closet in railroad cars. This pivoted bottom closed automatically by the raising of the seat cover and opened automatically by the closing of that cover.

In 1880 Latimer was hired as a draftsman by Hiram Maxim, chief engineer for the United States

[1]U.S. Patent number 147,363.

Electric Lighting Company, then located in Bridge-port, Connecticut. At that time the electric industry was in its youth. A year before, in 1879, Thomas Edison had invented the incandescent electric lamp that was to usher in a new age of electric lighting in the country and later in the world. Latimer became an important part of the electrical world. He studied all aspects of electricity in his precise and thorough manner. He carried on experiments which resulted in improvements on the incandescent lamp, particularly in the ways in which the carbon filaments were made and mounted. The Latimer lamp that resulted was in wide use for some time.

On September 13, 1881, Latimer and Joseph V. Nichols received a patent for their "Electric Lamp."[2] Their invention dealt with the method of mounting the carbons or connecting them to the metal wires in the lamp. Part of the description in the patent states: "Our invention relates to electric lamps in which the light is produced by the incandescence of a continuous strip of carbon secured to metallic wires and enclosed in a hermetically sealed and thoroughly exhausted transparent receiver; and it relates more especially to the method of mounting the carbons or connecting them with the wires."

[2] U.S. Patent number 247,097.

It was on January 17, 1882, that Latimer received what was probably his most important patent, a "Process of Manufacturing Carbons."[3] The carbon filaments that were used in Edison's lamps were made of various materials, including bamboo, which were exposed to high heat in the absence of air. This resulted in the material being reduced to filaments of carbon that were then used in the incandescent lamp. Latimer's method for producing carbon filaments resulted in a superior filament that lasted much longer. In his method, shapes or blanks were cut out of fibrous or textile materials that were then placed under pressure between sheets or envelopes of cardboard whose rate of expansion and contraction when exposed to heat was the same as the materials used. This patent was assigned by Latimer to his employer, the U.S. Electric Lighting Company, located by that time in New York City.

Another of Latimer's inventions assigned to the same company was the "Globe Supporter for Electric Lamps"[4] patented on March 21, 1882. This dealt with a globe or shade holder for electric arc lamps which permitted the "passage of the carbons and was provided with end clasps to the side rods of the

[3] U.S. Patent number 252,386.
[4] U.S. Patent number 255,212.

lamp which receive and clasp between them the globe." Wooden electric-lamp sockets designed and made by Latimer are now on display in the Smithsonian Institution in Washington, D.C.

It was not long before Latimer was called upon to install some of the first Maxim incandescent electric light plants in New York City. He installed electric lighting in the Equitable Building, the Union League Club of New York City, and other buildings. Today New York City and other large cities glitter at night like thousands of jewels in a vast setting. From New York to California, the cities of this country shine in the night. This brilliance, taken for granted today, was made possible by the pioneering work of men such as Edison and Latimer. Like television, radio, steam heat, and electric alarm clocks, the incandescent light that illuminates our homes and streets and highways is just another convenience of our times. And it all started only a little more than one hundred years ago.

At the time Latimer was helping to light it up, New York City was very different from what it is today. The Brooklyn Bridge was just being put into operation, and commuters from Brooklyn, Queens, and Long Island came by ferry. Sailing ships and steamboats dotted the rivers and harbor. The Tribune Building, one of the tallest, was just ten stories high. Getting downtown to work involved a ride on a horse-drawn trolley or on one of the four steam-engined elevated lines which ran on Second, Third, Sixth, and Ninth Avenues. Your white shirt might be spotted with coal dust from flying cinders by the time you reached your destination. If you went downtown by horse-drawn carriage, the traffic tangled as wagons carrying food, clothes, and materials converged with streetcars and carriages in the narrow streets. Overhead, the telephone and telegraph wires looked like endless strands of black clothesline.

If you worked in a factory, you were probably so worn out after a sixteen-hour day that you went to sleep right after dinner. If you were one of the recent immigrants from southern Europe, your home was probably a crowded single room, shared by another family, on the Lower East Side. The 1880s, however, were not entirely without their good points. Free lunch went with every schooner of nickel beer, store clerks were polite, and there was no income tax.

In those days electric arc lamps were used to light up the streets. These lamps were wired in a series circuit. You may recall from your science class that in a series circuit, if one lamp goes out, all the lamps go out. Latimer wired his incandescent lamps in a parallel circuit so that if one lamp went out, the others would continue to give light. He went on to install electric lighting in Philadelphia and in Canada, where he had to learn to speak French in order to explain his orders to the Canadian workers.

In the autumn of 1881, Latimer was sent to London to set up an incandescent lamp department for the Maxim-Weston Electric Light Company. There he supervised the production of the carbon filaments by the method he had invented. He knew more about it than anyone else in the business. He took his wife with him and together they enjoyed a delayed honeymoon. English businessmen, however, were not accustomed to being told what to do by an employee, much less a black employee, and Latimer wrote in his diary, "In London I was in hot water from the day I came until I returned." But his mission was carried out successfully.

On his return from London, Latimer was employed by the Olmstead Electric Lighting Company of Brooklyn and then by the Acme Electric Light Company of New York City. It was in 1884 that the call came from Thomas Edison, and Latimer became associated with the Engineering Department of the Edison Electric Light Company at 65 Fifth Avenue in New York City. In 1890 he was transferred to the Legal Department, where he was of tremendous value to Edison in defending his patents in court as an expert witness. Millions of dollars hinged upon his testimony and such was the stature of Latimer's knowledge of the electrical industry that more often than not his expert testimony won the case for Edison.

In the meantime, the Edison Electric Light Company became the General Electric Company of today. In 1896 the General Electric and Westinghouse Companies together formed the Board of Patent Control to protect their patents against encroachments by other companies. Latimer became the board's chief draftsman and expert witness, a position he held until the abolition of the board in 1911. At that time he became associated with Edwin W. Hammer, a New York City engineer, and later with the firm of Hammer & Schwarz. Hammer had been an assistant in Edison's laboratory and started a collection of the various types of incandescent lamps. The Hammer Collection is now on exhibit in Detroit, Michigan, and among its more than eight hundred lamps is the Latimer lamp.

In 1890 Latimer wrote the standard book on electric lighting[5] in which he describes the way in

[5]Lewis H. Latimer, *Incandescent Electric Lighting. A Practical Description of the Edison System* (New York: D. Van Nostrand Company, 1890).

which light is obtained by heating an electric wire to incandescence. After describing the electric lamp itself, he gives the following account of the principles involved:

If the electric current can be forced through a substance that is a poor conductor, it will create a degree of heat in that substance which will be greater or less according to the quantity of electricity through it. Upon this principle of the heating effect of the electric current is based the operation of the incandescent lamp just described. While the copper and platinum wires readily conduct the current, the carbon filament offers a great deal of resistance to its passage and for this reason becomes very hot, in fact is raised to white heat or incandescence, which gives its name to the lamp. You doubtless wonder why this thread of charcoal is not immediately consumed when in this state, but this is readily accounted for when you remember that without the oxygen of the air there can be no combustion, and that every possible trace of air has been removed from the bulb and it is so thoroughly sealed up as to prevent the admission of the air about it; and yet the lamp does not last forever, for the reason that the action of the current upon the carbon has a tendency to divide up its particles and transfer them from one filament to another so that, sooner or later, the filament gives way at some point.

Latimer's activities were brought to a conclusion in the early part of 1924 by an illness that finally caused his death on December 11, 1928. On his death, the Edison Pioneers, an organization made up of those scientists who actually worked with Thomas Edison in his pioneering work in the field of electricity, paid tribute to him:

We hardly mourn his inevitable going so much as we rejoice in pleasant memory at having been associated with him in a great work for all people under a great man.

He was of the colored race, the only one in our organization, and was one of those to respond to the initial call that led to the formation of the Edison Pioneers, January 24, 1918. Broad-mindedness, versatility in the accomplishment of things intellectual and cultural, a linguist, a devoted husband and father, all were characteristic of him, and his genial presence will be missed from our gatherings.

Mr. Latimer was a full member, and an esteemed one, of the

Edison Pioneers

On November 9, 1929, the *New York Age* carried an article stating, "One of the interesting features in connection with the recent Light's Golden Jubilee, celebrating the fiftieth anniversary of Thomas A. Edison's invention of the electric light, was the presence of two daughters of the late Lewis Howard Latimer, the only colored member of the Edison Pioneers, the group of workers who were associated with Edison in the development of his electrical invention." In 1954, however, when the seventy-fifth anniversary of Edison's invention was being celebrated, no mention was made of the role played by Lewis Latimer. His two daughters were guests of honor at the fiftieth anniversary celebration. What happened by 1954—the seventy-fifth anniversary? Was the only black member of the Edison Pioneers already forgotten?

Latimer's inventive genius was not confined to the field of electricity. On January 12, 1886, he was awarded a patent for an "Apparatus for Cooling

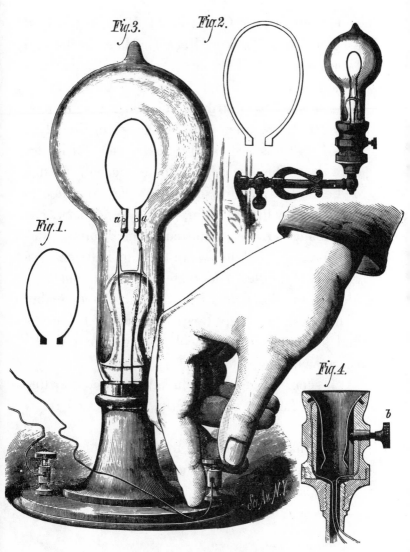

The incandescent lamp

and Disinfecting."[6] On March 24, 1896, he received a patent for a "Locking Rack for Hats, Coats, and Umbrellas."[7] On February 7, 1905, a patent was issued to him for "Book Supports."[8]

The most recent tribute to Latimer was given on May 10, 1968, when a public school in Brooklyn, New York, was dedicated to his memory. It is now known as The Lewis H. Latimer School. At this dedication, a painting of Latimer was presented to the school by his grandson, Gerald Norman, Sr. His granddaughter, Miss Winifred Latimer Norman, was also present. Tributes were paid to Latimer by a member of the New York State Legislature, the President of the Borough of Brooklyn, and by a member of the New York City Board of Education. Parents and students of the school also took part in the ceremony.

It seems fitting to conclude with a poem written by Lewis Latimer called "Drink to the Dead":

> Drink now in silence to the dead;
> Those noble souls who've passed away,
> Whose promise like the withered flower
> Was quenched in premature decay.

[6] U.S. Patent number 334,078.
[7] U.S. Patent number 557,076.
[8] U.S. Patent number 781,890.

Fill up your glasses to the brim;
They would not have our joy the less
Than when they sat among us here,
In all their youth and joyousness.
Drink to the souls now passed beyond;
And be our thoughts from sorrow free;
Ring out the praise of those great souls,
In one grand earnest symphony;
So that in time, when we are gone,
The Living may our praise proclaim,
And loving lips drink unto us,
To keep alive fond memory's flame.

Garrett A. Morgan
1877–1963

Men trapped in mines or tunnels? Garrett Morgan to the rescue! Soldiers attacked by poison gas on the battlefield? Garrett Morgan to the rescue! You have heard of the gas mask. Have you heard of its inventor?

Garrett A. Morgan was born in Paris, Kentucky, on March 4, 1877. He was the seventh of a family of eleven children. His father, Sydney Morgan, was a mulatto. His mother, Elizabeth Reed Morgan, a former slave who received her freedom in 1863, was of mixed Negro and Indian blood.

Garrett received an elementary school education in his home town but he had no further formal education. He left home at the age of fourteen and went to Cincinnati, Ohio, where he worked as general handyman for a white landowner. Because of the lack of opportunity, Garrett went on to Cleveland, where he was to spend the rest of his life. He

Garrett A. Morgan, pioneer in safety

arrived in Cleveland on a beautiful day in June, 1895, full of hope, but with only one dime in his pocket.

In Cleveland he taught himself enough about the sewing machine to secure a job as machine adjuster with Roots and McBride and later with other companies. By 1907 he decided to work for himself and opened a shop that sold and repaired sewing machines. Here he earned enough money to buy his own home and he sent for his mother, who had lost her husband. One year later he married Mary Anne Hassek, with whom he was to share his life for fifty-five years until his death in 1963. It was a very happy marriage and Morgan was blessed with three sons and seven grandchildren.[1]

In 1909 Morgan opened a tailoring shop that manufactured dresses, suits, and coats. It was a large shop employing thirty-two workers. It was at this time that chance brought about Morgan's first invention. He was working on a problem that had come up in connection with the sewing of woolens by sewing machines. The needle of the sewing machine moved up and down so quickly that it frequently scorched the thread of the woolen material by the heat of friction. Morgan was experimenting at home with a chemical solution that could be applied to the needle to reduce the friction and eliminate the scorching. When his wife called him to come to dinner, he wiped the solution from his hands onto a piece of wiry pony-fur cloth that was lying

[1]His eldest son, John Pierpont Morgan, served with the city of Cleveland's Recreation Department for thirty years. Garrett Augustus Morgan, Jr., is the supervisor of the Cuyahoga County Detention Home. The youngest son, Cosmo Henry Morgan, is a pharmacist.

around. When he returned from dinner, Morgan noticed that the wiry fuzz of the cloth where he had wiped his hands was quite straight. The chemical solution had apparently caused the fuzzy hairs to straighten out. Morgan saw the possibilities and decided to try it out. His next-door neighbor had an Airedale dog. Morgan set to work on the dog's hair with his chemical solution. It did such a perfect job of hair straightening that when the dog returned home, his master drove out the "strange" dog. He did not recognize his own dog in his new "hairdo." Morgan then tried the solution on his own hair, a little at a time, then gradually the whole head. Thus was born the first human hair straightener, which was marketed as the G. A. Morgan Hair Refining Cream. Today the G. A. Morgan Refining Company, organized in 1913, is still located in its original building at 5204 Harlem Avenue in Cleveland and is still doing a thriving business.

It was in 1912 that Morgan came out with his most important invention, the Safety Hood, later to become known as the gas mask. In his application for a patent, Morgan referred to it as a "Breathing Device." The patent was granted in 1914 (U.S. Patent number 1,113,675). The device consisted of a hood placed over the head of the user. A tube from this hood was provided with an inlet opening for air, and the tube was long enough to enter a layer of air underneath the dense smoke or gas. This tube could then be placed beyond the reach of gas fumes and dust and through it pure air could be furnished to the user. The lower end of the tube was lined for some distance with an absorbent material such as sponge which was moistened with water before use. This served to prevent the smoke and dust from going up the tube, and also served to cool the air. There was a separate tube containing a valve for exhaled air.

In Morgan's words, "The object of the invention is to provide a portable attachment which will enable a fireman to enter a house filled with thick suffocating gases and smoke and to breathe freely for some time therein, and thereby enable him to perform his duties of saving life and valuables without danger to himself from suffocation. The device is also efficient and useful for protection to engineers, chemists, and working men who are obliged to breathe noxious fumes or dust derived from the materials in which they are obliged to work."

The National Safety Device Company was set up to manufacture and sell the Safety Hood, and Morgan was retained as the general manager. He was the only nonwhite officer in the company. It was interesting to note that for three months Morgan

1,113,675.

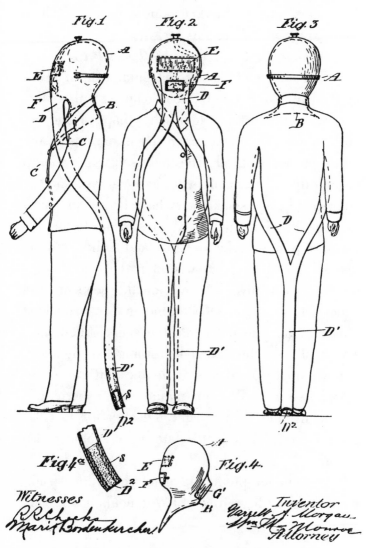

Fig.1   *Fig.2*   *Fig.3*

Fig.4ᵃ   *Fig.4.*

Witnesses
R. R. Cheeke
Marie Bordenkurcher

Inventor
Garrett A. Morgan
Wm. H. Monroe
Attorney

Garrett A. Morgan's breathing helmet

urged colored people to buy stock in this company at $10 per share, but his efforts were unsuccessful. Thirty days later the stock sold for $100 a share. Two years later its market value exceeded $250 a share and not a share was for sale.

On October 22, 1914, the *Times-Picayune* of New Orleans reported a spectacular exhibit given by the National Safety Device Company with a Morgan helmet. A canvas tent, close-flapped and secure, was erected on an open space, and inside the tent a fire was started. The fuel used was made up of tar sulphur, formaldehyde, and manure, and the character of the smoke was the thickest and most evil-smelling imaginable. Charles Salan, former director of public works for Cleveland, conducted the tests. Fitting a large canvas affair that had the appearance of a diver's helmet on the head of "Big Chief" Mason, a full-blooded Indian, Mr. Salan sent Mason under the flaps into the smoke-filled tent. The smoke was thick enough to strangle an elephant, but Mason lingered around in the suffocating atmosphere for a full twenty minutes and experienced no inconvenience. He came out after the test "as good as new," and a little later gave another exhibition.

Artificial ice-producing plants generally use ammonia gas as the refrigerant. Ammonia gas is very poisonous. In a letter from the Artificial Ice and Storage Company, the superintendent of the plant stated, "In regards to your G. A. Morgan Breathing Helmet, I wish to say that it was given a severe test in a small room eight feet by ten feet with a seven foot ceiling. Anhydrous (free of water) ammonia was forced into the room to a great extent. Mr. Mason, your demonstrator, put on the helmet and remained in the room for fifteen minutes. It seemed to have no apparent effect on him. I myself tried it and remained there for ten minutes and could have remained longer."

At the Second International Exposition of Safety and Sanitation in New York City in 1914, Morgan received a solid gold medal, the First Grand Prize, for his invention. On that occasion, several very successful demonstrations were made, and a practical demonstration was afforded the public when helmets were rushed from the exhibit booth by New York firemen for use in rescuing victims of a terrible subway disaster. It was not long before fire departments all over the country were using the Morgan Safety Hood with excellent results in terms of saving lives and property.

The crucial test of this invention came on July 24, 1916. On that day a disastrous explosion took place in the tunnel of Crib number five of the Cleveland Water Works, 250 feet below Lake Erie. The tunnel quickly filled with smoke, dust, and poisonous gases. Thirty-two men who had been working in the tunnel were trapped. If they could not be gotten out quickly, they would die of suffocation and gas. But it was suicide for anyone to enter that gas-and-smoke-filled tunnel to try to rescue them. Then someone remembered Morgan and his Safety Hood. Morgan was called and came running with his brother Frank. The two quickly put on their Safety Hoods and entered the tunnel. To the crowd of relatives and friends waiting at the entrance to the tunnel, it seemed like eternity. Grim-faced men and sobbing women were beginning to give up hope when suddenly a cheer went up. Morgan had emerged from the tunnel carrying an injured man on his back! He immediately reentered the tunnel for more. It is not known how many trips Morgan and his brother made into the tunnel that day, but when they had finished every one of the trapped men had been brought out, although not all were alive.

Newspapers all over the country carried the story of Morgan's heroism. He was given a solid gold, diamond-studded medal by a group of prominent citizens of Cleveland with the inscription, "To Garrett A. Morgan, our most honored and bravest citizen." He also received a medal from the International

Association of Fire Engineers and was made an honorary member of that association.

Requests came from fire departments, police departments, and mining companies asking for demonstrations of the Morgan Safety Hood. Morgan set up his own company to manufacture and sell the hoods. In the Deep South it became necessary for Morgan to employ a white man to show his invention. Orders began to pour in but stopped when it became known that the inventor was black.

During World War I, Morgan's Safety Hood was improved upon and emerged as the gas mask that the U.S. Army used so successfully on the battlefield to save the lives of thousands of our soldiers. It became part of the standard equipment of a soldier in the field. It was also used in subsequent wars.

It was not long before Morgan's fertile brain began to work on another safety device. One day he witnessed an accident involving an automobile and a horse and carriage. The two vehicles had collided at a street intersection. Two people were thrown out of the carriage and the driver of the automobile was knocked unconscious. The horse was badly injured and had to be shot. With the growing number of automobiles on the streets, Morgan felt that something had to be done to prevent such accidents. He thought about it a good deal and finally came up

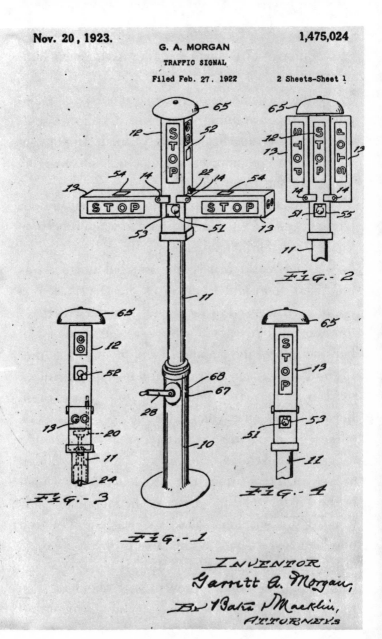

FIG.-2

FIG.-3

FIG.-1

FIG.-4

INVENTOR
Garrett A. Morgan,
By Baker Macklin,
ATTORNEYS

Garrett A. Morgan's traffic light signal

with an idea. Why not have electric light signals at intersections with different colored lights as signals for stopping or going? In this way accidents caused by cross traffic in the streets would be eliminated. Thus was born the first traffic light signal system which is now used all over the world.

Morgan patented his traffic signal in November, 1923 (U.S. Patent number 1,475,024), and secured British and Canadian patents as well. The rights to this traffic signal were sold by Morgan to the General Electric Corporation for the sum of $40,000, a truly large sum of money at that time. An exhibit of Morgan's traffic signal was held as recently as 1963, six months before his death, when he was cited by the U.S. Government for inventing the first traffic signal.

Morgan was a jolly man, although he had his sterner moments. He was quick-tempered and outspoken, which often made enemies for him. However, his great warmth and good nature brought him many friends, including John D. Rockefeller, Sr., and J. Pierpont Morgan, the financier, after whom he named his eldest son. He was a lover of the out-of-doors and did a great deal of hunting and fishing when he had the chance. Morgan's genius was not confined to any one area. Besides the inventions referred to, he also invented a woman's hat fastener, a round belt fastener, and a friction drive clutch.

Garrett A. Morgan with his son and grandson

That Morgan was concerned about the welfare of black people is shown in many ways. For example, he was concerned about the lack of coverage of Negro affairs in the Cleveland newspapers. He decided to start his own newspaper which would contain news about Negroes in Cleveland and all over the country. The *Cleveland Call* was the result. The name was later changed to the *Call & Post* and the paper is now published in Cleveland, Columbus, and Cincinnati. It has a large circulation.

Morgan served as treasurer of the Cleveland Association of Colored Men from 1914 until it merged with the National Association for the Advancement of Colored People. He remained an active member of the NAACP all of his life.

In 1931 Morgan decided to run as an independent candidate for the City Council in Cleveland. He felt that the black man was not being properly represented. In a campaign speech he promised: "If elected, I will try to lead the people of the third district to EQUAL representation in the affairs of city government." It is of interest to note that thirty-seven years later we had Mayor Stokes of Cleveland, the first black man to become mayor of a large city in the United States. Did Morgan prepare the ground for Stokes' success? The platform on which Morgan

ran could well be the platform today. It included
the following:

1. Relief for the unemployed and a more economic and efficient administration of public
   affairs.
2. Improved housing conditions.
3. Better lighting and policing and improved
   sanitation.
4. Improved city-owned hospital accommoda-
   tions.

In 1943 Morgan developed glaucoma, an eye
disease, as a result of which he lost 90 percent of
his sight. He was operated on at the Mayo Clinic
and made yearly visits thereafter to the Clinic. Despite his near-blindness, Morgan made constant use
of his mind and hands and always kept busy. His
last goal in life was to be able to attend the Emancipation Centennial, which was to be held in Chicago in August, 1963. It was not to be. After two
years of illness, on July 27, 1963, Morgan died at
the age of eighty-six, one month before the Centennial was to take place. He did receive national recognition at the Centennial. His wife, Mary, died five
years later at the age of eighty-four.

Morgan's life was a long, happy, and extremely

useful one. His contributions are felt not only in our country but throughout the world. The world is a safer place because of his work. Can you picture the streets of a large city of modern times without the safety of traffic light signals? Do you know of the many uses gas masks are put to besides being used in warfare? Industrial uses are many. The U.S. Public Health Service uses special gas masks in fumigating public buildings with cyanide gas to kill rodents and roaches.

Morgan was a self-educated and a creative man. When one examines the complicated and often technological nature of his work, one wonders how it could have come from an individual whose only formal education ended in the elementary school. It is the remarkable achievement of a truly remarkable man.

George Washington Carver
1860–1943

On January 6, 1943, a telegram was sent by Franklin D. Roosevelt, the President of the United States, to the Tuskegee Institute. It read: "The world of science has lost one of its most eminent figures and the race from which he sprang an outstanding member in the passing of Dr. George Washington Carver. The versatility of his genius and his achievements in diverse branches of the arts and sciences were truly amazing. All mankind are the beneficiaries of his discoveries in the field of agricultural chemistry. The things which he achieved in the face of early handicaps will for all time afford an inspiring example to youth everywhere. I count it a great privilege to have met Dr. Carver and to have talked with him at Tuskegee on the happy occasion of my visit to the Institute which was the scene of his long and distinguished labors."

George Washington Carver, agricultural chemist

It was Carver who revolutionized and revitalized the dying agriculture of the South. Because of his efforts, the peanut crop alone brought the South an income of sixty million dollars in a single year!

Born of slave parents on the plantation of Moses Carver near Diamond Grove in Missouri, he and his mother were stolen one night by a band of night raiders. His mother was never recovered but the half-dead infant was ransomed in exchange for a racing horse. The year was 1860.

Miraculously, the sickly slave baby recovered. As he grew up, it soon became clear that he had an unusually good mind. His early love and knowledge of plants, his thirst for knowledge, and his determination to become a scientist was to make him one of the most honored men of his time.

Since there were no schools near the Carver farm, he was sent to Neosho, the Newton County seat in southwest Missouri, where he worked as a farm hand and studied in a one-room, one-teacher school. From there he went on to the Minneapolis High School in Kansas, where his record was so outstanding that when he mailed an application to the Highland University in Kansas he was accepted with a scholarship. In a very happy frame of mind, young Carver went there to register. When he showed up in person, the president of the university took one look at him and demanded, "Why didn't you tell me you were a Negro?" Carver was turned away.

Disillusioned but determined, he worked on the land and saved money for the time when he could go on with his education. Fortune smiled at last, and in 1887 he was accepted by Simpson College, a Methodist school in Indianola, Iowa, where he supported himself by ironing the shirts, darning the socks, and patching up the clothing of his fellow students. At Simpson he showed considerable talent in art, and was encouraged by his art teacher, Miss Etta Budd, who felt he should go to Paris for further training in art. Twenty-seven of the oil paintings now hanging in the Carver Art Collection were done at Simpson. However, Carver was intent on a science career and soon the laboratories at Simpson proved to be inadequate for his needs. It was then, in 1891, that he left Simpson College and entered Iowa Agricultural College (now the Iowa State University) at Ames, Iowa, with the finest recommendations from Simpson.

At Iowa Agricultural College the departments of botany and agricultural chemistry were excellent, and Carver did some outstanding work there. One of his teachers, James Wilson, who was director of the U.S. Experimental Station at the College, was later to become a secretary in President Theodore

Roosevelt's cabinet. Another of his teachers was Henry Wallace, Sr., the father of Henry Wallace, Jr., who was to become Secretary of Agriculture and later Vice-President of the United States under President Franklin D. Roosevelt. There was a lifelong and warm friendship between Carver and the younger Wallace.

When he graduated from Iowa Agricultural College with a B.S. degree in 1894 he was hailed as one of Iowa's outstanding scholars and was given an appointment on the faculty—the first black man to serve on that faculty. During his studies at Iowa, Carver still found time to paint and in 1893 four of his paintings were selected to hang in the Art Exhibit at the World's Columbian Exposition.

While teaching agriculture and bacterial botany, and taking charge of the greenhouses, Carver also pursued graduate work, and his studies included research and experimentation. His earliest scientific contribution was his investigation of ferns, which he reported in a paper[1] that gave the conditions under which they grew in the North. Together with his teacher, Louis Hermann Pammell, an eminent botanist, Carver conducted experiments in plant pathology (diseases of plants). In 1895 the two men

[1] Iowa State College, *Agricultural Bulletin*, no. 27, 1895, pp. 150–153.

published significant results on the prevention and cure of certain fungus diseases that destroyed cherry and currant plants. Carver also conducted special investigations of several species of rust (a fungus) that attacked and destroyed wheat, oats, blackberry, and carnations. Other experiments in this period of his life dealt with problems of types of soil, moisture, sunlight, rooting, cuttings, and reproduction of plants.

By 1896 Carver received a master's degree (M.S.) in Agriculture and was already making important discoveries in the field of plant pathology. In 1897 he reported, for the first time in America, a new species of Taphrina, a fungus found to grow on red and silver maple trees. Later this species of Taphrina was named *Taphrina Carveri*.[2] Two other fungi that were first discovered by Carver were named after him: *Collectotrichum Carveri* and *Metasphaeria Carveri*. He was also the first in America to observe and report on a fungus growth that caused a disease of the soybean.

Just when it seemed that Carver was settling down to a long and promising scientific career at Iowa, a letter came from Booker T. Washington of the Tuskegee Normal and Industrial Institute for

[2] A. E. Jenkins, *Journal of Washington Academy of Science*, vol. 29, May 15, 1939, p. 282.

Negroes, telling Carver how desperately he was needed at Tuskegee by his people. In reply, Carver wrote simply, "I am coming." He was to remain there for the rest of his life and the things he accomplished there have become known to the world.

At Tuskegee, Carver was made first director of agriculture, a high-sounding title not in keeping with the situation he found. For his research there was only a barren piece of land devoid of any signs of a laboratory. He was also director of the Research and Experiment Station there, established by an act of the State Legislature in 1896. With the twenty-acre patch of unbelievably poor land assigned to him, Carver and his students planted cowpeas, a legume. Legumes are plants that have nitrogen-fixing bacteria on their roots. These bacteria take nitrogen from the air and convert it into nitrates, which are held by the soil as fertilizer. The soil thereby becomes enriched. He then planted sweet potatoes and then cotton. By the time he planted the cotton, the soil had become so enriched that he was able to harvest five hundred pounds of cotton for every acre of land. The farmers in the area were greatly impressed. Their land never produced anywhere near that amount of cotton.

By his demonstration with that patch of land,

Carver impressed upon the farmers the need for "crop rotation." Since cotton, tobacco, and other plants took the nitrates out of the soil, thereby impoverishing it, these nitrates had to be put back in order to enrich the soil. They could be put back by legumes such as peanuts, clover, peas, and so on. By this method, crops were rotated: first a crop of legumes, then a crop of cotton or tobacco. "Plant peanuts," Carver told the farmers. "They are excellent legumes, they enrich the soil, they are easy to plant, easy to grow, and easy to harvest, they are rich in protein and good for feeding livestock, they yield a high percentage of oil of a superior quality. A pound of peanuts contains a little more of the bodybuilding nutrients than a pound of sirloin steak."

Seeing his graphically successful example, the farmers in the South turned to planting peanuts and the results were far beyond their expectations. The cotton and tobacco crops that followed were the best they had ever had. However, despite using peanuts for feeding cattle, the farmers' warehouses soon began to fill to overflowing with peanuts that they could not sell and that had begun to rot. What were they going to do? They were angry with Carver and felt that he had tricked them into planting the peanuts. Carver went back to the laboratory that had been painfully fitted up with bottles, old kitchen utensils, containers of all kinds, tops of cans, and other materials retrieved from scrap heaps.

In one week's time, Carver had discovered about two dozen products that could be obtained from the peanut, such as milk and cheese. He went on to work on more products from peanuts in his laboratory in later years and wound up eventually with 325 different products, including cream, buttermilk, instant coffee, face powder, printer's ink, butter, shampoo, vinegar, dyes, soap, and wood stains.[3]

Soon many industries sprang up that made use of these peanut products and it wasn't long before farmers were getting more money for their peanut crop than for their cotton or tobacco crops. The South began to prosper because of this black scientist's genius.

Carver now turned his attention to the sweet potato and discovered 118 products that could be made from it, such as flour, starch, tapioca, dyes, ink, mucilage, and synthetic rubber. In fact, during World War I, the U.S. Army used his sweet potato to mix with wheat flour to make a better and cheaper

[3] G. W. Carver, "Many Food Products Can Be Made from Peanuts and Sweet Potato," American Food Journal, August, 1921.

loaf of bread. This was particularly important because of the shortage of wheat during the war.[4]

From the pecan, a plant that grew well in the South, he extracted seventy-five different products, as well as hundreds of products from waste material such as corn stalks. When there was an overabundance of cotton, Carver showed how it could be used to make insulating board, paper, rugs, cordage, and paving blocks for highways.

From the native clays of Alabama, Carver extracted some of the most beautiful dyes and paints. When aniline dyes from Germany became unavailable during the war, Carver's clay dyes were widely used and proved to be superior to the aniline dyes. The distinguished chemist, Wade Moss, lauded Carver for his discovery of a new synthesis of organic dyes extracted from the soils of Macon County in Alabama.[5]

In 1921 an interesting event took place. Carver had been asked by the peanut growers in the South to testify before the Ways and Means Committee of the U.S. House of Representatives in favor of a tariff to protect the peanut from foreign competition. He

[4] G. W. Carver, "The Undiscovered Sweet Potato," *Agricultural Digest*, vol. 2, no. 11, April, 1918.

[5] W. Moss, *Manufacturers Record*, vol. 98, July 24, 1930, p. 58.

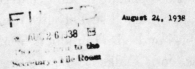

August 24, 1938

Dr. G. W. Carver
Director, Agricultural Research and
   Experiment Station
Tuskegee Institute, Alabama

Dear Dr. Carver:

Thanks so much for sending me your letter of August 18.
I will get in touch with our Bureau of Plant Industry people
at once and get their advice on Sida Spinoso.

It is good to know that your work is going to be so
effectively preserved for posterity.

The other day I was interested in seeing you in the
movies. You looked so unusually well.

Sincerely yours,

secretary's File Room
(Signed)

H a Wallace

Secretary

Letter from Henry A. Wallace, Secretary of Agriculture under
President Franklin D. Roosevelt and later Vice-President,
to George W. Carver, dated August 24, 1938

was given ten minutes to make his presentation.
Carrying a huge suitcase full of samples, he demonstrated some of the many products he had made
from the peanut, and explained how they could be
used and why they were valuable. When his ten

minutes were up, the members of the Committee were so fascinated by what they saw that they urged him to continue, which he did for more than an hour. Afterward, he was complimented by the chairman of the Committee on his presentation and his knowledge, and the peanut was included in the Hawley-Smoot Tariff Bill as a result.[6]

Records in the National Archives in Washington, D.C., contain the correspondence during this time of Carver with many scientists and government officials, including Secretary of Agriculture Henry Wallace.[7] These records proved to be very informative as well as interesting to the author.

Honors for Carver's outstanding work began to come in. In 1916 he was elected a Fellow of the Royal Society of Arts, Manufactures and Commerce of Great Britain, an honor given to few Americans. In 1923, he was awarded the Spingarn Medal.[8] In

[6]G. W. Carver, Statement at Hearings before the Committee on Ways and Means, House of Representatives, Schedule G, Agricultural Products and Provisions, January 21, 1921, Tariff Information, 1921 (Washington, D.C.: Government Printing Office, 1921), p. 1599.

[7]National Archives, Washington, D.C., General Records, Agriculture Department, 1839–1943 (RG 16). Office of Experiment Stations, 1888–1937 (RG 164).

[8]Awarded annually by the National Association for the Advancement of Colored People to "the man or woman of African descent who will have made the highest achievement during the preceding year or years in any honorable field of human endeavor."

1939, he received the Theodore Roosevelt Medal "for distinguished research in agricultural chemistry." The medal was accompanied by the following citation: "To a scientist humbly seeking the guidance of God and a liberator to the men of the white race as well as the black."

Besides being visited by prominent scientists from this and other countries, Carver also played host to the Crown Prince of Sweden and the British Prince of Wales, both of whom showed profound interest in his work with the peanut. He was invited by Thomas Edison to join his staff at Orange Grove, New Jersey, with an offer of unlimited laboratory facilities and a salary of more than one hundred thousand dollars a year! He received a similar offer from the automobile pioneer, Henry Ford. Both offers were turned down with thanks. Tuskegee needed him more.

Henry Ford came to Tuskegee to meet Carver and the two became friends. Carver visited Ford in Dearborn, Michigan, where Ford had gone into development and experimentation with soybeans. When Carver returned to his laboratory, he developed a plastic material from soybeans which Ford was able to make use of in certain parts of his automobile. Later, Ford and Carver worked together on using

TUSKEGEE NORMAL AND INDUSTRIAL INSTITUTE

FOUNDED BY BOOKER T. WASHINGTON

FOR THE TRAINING OF COLORED YOUNG MEN AND WOMEN

RESEARCH AND EXPERIMENT STATION
GEORGE W. CARVER, DIRECTOR

TUSKEGEE INSTITUTE, ALABAMA

Aug. 20 - 33.

Hon. H. A. Wallace.

Secy. of Agr.

Washington. D.C.

My dear Mr. Secy:-

This is just to extend to you greetings, acknowledge receipt of your letter bearing the good news that you, "Bobby" and Dr. Scofield reached Washington safely.

I am looking forward to my H. A. Wallace. Jr. Collection of Amaryllis with much pleasure as the ties which cluster around these Collections are sacred to me.

The other day when down town I was made especially happy when your name was being discussed by a group of very prominent people. They said you were the most promiseing Presidential "timber" in sight for next time.

With much love and good wishes.

G. W. Carver.

Letter from George W. Carver to Secretary of Agriculture
Henry A. Wallace, dated August 20, 1933

the plant weed, goldenrod, for producing synthetic rubber.

In 1934, Carver was appointed collaborator in the Mycology and Plant Disease Survey undertaken by the Bureau of Plant Industry of the U.S. Department of Agriculture. Mycology is the branch of biology dealing with the study of fungi and Carver was glad to get back to some of his earlier work dealing with diseases in plants caused by fungi.

In 1940, Carver was chosen "man of the year" and given a plaque by the International Federation of Architects, Engineers, Chemists and Technicians as having "contributed most to science" and for his "distinguished service to humanity." In 1928 he had received the honorary degree of Doctor of Science (Sc.D.) from his alma mater, Simpson College. In 1941 he received a similar degree from the University of Rochester.

In later years, when the gifted artist Betsy Graves Reyneau came to Tuskegee to paint Carver, it was not a portrait of the usual kind. She "wanted to catch him at his work." This she did beautifully by painting him with an amaryllis, a flower with which he had been working for years. His long, sensitive fingers show up beautifully in the painting as he handles the flower. (See page 105.)

Because of the pressures of his work and his

advancing years, Carver's strength began to give out. A fall on an icy street on a cold winter day confined him to bed, from which he did not arise. He died on the Tuskegee campus, his home for the past fifty years, on January 5, 1943. Three months later, on April 18, 1943, he was honored posthumously by being awarded the New York City Teachers Union Medal, Local 5.

Statements have been made that Carver always refused to patent any of his inventions. A search of the records of the U.S. Patent Office, however, reveals that Carver was granted three patents, one for a process of making cosmetic preparations from peanuts,[9] another giving him blanket patents covering several processes for the manufacture of paints and stains from clays and minerals,[10] and a third for an improved method of producing paints and stains which includes a cold-water process.[11]

Carver had never married or had any family ties. When he died, he left his life savings—the sum of $33,000—to establish the George Washington Carver Foundation to help provide research opportunities for scientists at Tuskegee. A memorial was erected in his honor at Tuskegee along with the Carver

[9]U.S. Patent number 1,522,176, January 6, 1925.
[10]U.S. Patent number 1,541,478, June 9, 1925.
[11]U.S. Patent number 1,632,365, June 14, 1927.

Museum, which holds thousands of mementos attesting to the love and esteem in which he was held all over the world. Here also is to be found a wide variety of exhibits that give some idea of the versatility and industry of Dr. Carver: paints, stains, and varnishes from Alabama clay; artificial marble from wood shavings; beautiful wall hangings from feed sacks and wrapping string; rugs and mats from weed fiber; and charming landscapes from water colors that started off as coffee grounds and orange peels.

In the Carver Art Collection room, the visitor can see his oil paintings. One of his paintings, "The Three Peaches," was done with his fingers, using the pigments he developed from Alabama clays. It was purchased by the Luxemberg Galleries in Paris.

The farmland near Diamond Grove, Missouri, where Carver was born and raised, is now maintained as a national monument by the U.S. Government.

A joint resolution of Congress, approved December 28, 1945 (Public Law 290 of the 79th Congress), designated January 5, 1946, as George Washington Carver Day with the following proclamation by President Truman:

"Whereas it is fitting that we honor the memory of George Washington Carver, who contributed to the expansion of the agricultural economy of the nation through his diligent research as an agricultural chemist, and

"Whereas by a joint resolution approved December 28, 1945, the Congress has designated January 5, 1946, as George Washington Carver Day and has authorized and requested me to issue a proclamation calling upon officials of the government to display the flag of the United States on all government buildings on such a day,

"Now, therefore, I, Harry S. Truman, President of the United States of America, do hereby call upon the officials of the Government to have the flag of the United States displayed on all Government buildings on January 5, 1946, in commemoration of the achievements of George Washington Carver."

Percy Lavon Julian
1899–1975

Millions of sufferers from arthritis, a crippling disease, owe their comfort and health to the "soybean chemist" who brought the healing drug cortisone within their reach. His outstanding contributions to the field of organic chemistry include the synthesis of the drug physostigmine and the extraction of important hormones from the soybean.

The grandson of a former slave, Percy Julian was born on April 11, 1899. He was one of a family of six children whose father, James Sumner Julian, was a railway mail clerk. That a good education was part of the Julian family tradition is shown by the fact that his two brothers went on to become physicians and his three sisters all won master's degrees. And the former Anna Johnson, whom Julian married on December 24, 1935, earned the degree of Doctor of Philosophy (Ph.D.) and was a practicing sociologist.

Percy Lavon Julian, soybean chemist

Julian went to elementary school in Montgomery, Alabama. One day he came home from school proudly waving an arithmetic examination paper marked "80." The elder Julian, ordinarily a kind man, scolded his son and told him, "Never be satisfied with mediocrity. That's what a grade of 80 is. After this, make it 100." Percy Julian batted 100 percent for the rest of his life.

With only one public high school in Birmingham for the hundreds of thousands of black children in all of Alabama, Julian was sent to the State Normal School for Negroes, a private school, in Montgomery, Alabama. When he graduated in 1916, he was admitted to DePauw University in Greencastle, Indiana. One of the scenes etched in Dr. Julian's memory was the day he left home to enroll at DePauw. From his seat in the train he looked out of the window and waved good-bye to his family. There stood his ninety-nine-year-old grandmother, who once had picked a record 350 pounds of cotton in one day; his grandfather, waving a hand from which two fingers were missing—cut off because his master discovered he had learned to write; and his father, whose waving hand seemed to say, "Make it 100, son."

His high school training had been so poor that he was admitted on probation as a "subfreshman," and for his first two years in school, he carried high school courses along with a full program of freshman and sophomore work. He slept in the attic of a white fraternity house where he worked as a waiter on tables. In spite of these handicaps, Julian went on to graduate at the top of his class, winning membership in the Phi Beta Kappa and Sigma Xi honorary societies. He was the valedictorian of the class of 1920.

Together with many of his fellow students, Julian wanted to go on to graduate study. It was the tradition in those days—and still is—for the head of the department to find graduate fellowships for the majors who wished to go on to the Ph.D. degree. But race prejudice was to dictate otherwise. In a book published in the 1960s Julian stated:

I shall never forget a week of anxious waiting in 1920 to see if I could get to graduate school. I had worked hard for four years. I stood by as day by day my fellow students in Chemistry came by saying, "I am going to Illinois"; "I am going to Ohio State"; "I am going to Michigan"; "I am going to Yale." "Where are you going?" they asked, and they answered for me, "You must be getting the Harvard plum." I could stand the suspense no longer. I went to Professor Blanchard, as staunch a friend as he knew how to be then, and certainly later my most unforgettable friend, and asked timidly, "Professor, did you get me a fellowship?" And then this dear fellow with resignation told me, "Now, now,

Julian, I knew you would be asking me that. Come into my office." There he showed me numerous letters from men who had really meant "God" to me—great American chemists of their day. And they had written to him, "I'll take your Mr.————, but I'd advise you to discourage your bright colored lad. We couldn't get him a job when he's done, and it'll only mean frustration. In industry, research demands co-work, and white boys would so sabotage his work that an industrial research leader would go crazy! And, of course, we couldn't find him a job as a teacher in a white university. Why don't you find him a teaching job in a Negro college in the South? He doesn't need a Ph.D. for that!" There went my dreams and hopes of four years, and as I pressed my lips to hold back the tears, I remembered my breeding, braced myself, and thanked him for thinking of me.[1]

Julian had wanted to be a chemist from the day when, as a small boy in Montgomery, a policeman pulled him down from a fence where he had been watching young white boys at work in a chemistry

[1]Stanton L. Wormley and L. H. Fenderson (editors), *Many Shades of Black* (New York: William Morrow & Company, 1969).

class in a high school that Negroes could not attend. He took Blanchard's advice and went to Fisk University, a Negro college, to teach chemistry. Two years later, he won the Austin Fellowship in Chemistry at Harvard University. There he established a brilliant scholastic record, getting straight A's and achieving the top group in his class. He received a master's degree in 1923 but was not offered the job of teaching assistant that was usually given to students with his standing. It was feared that Southern students might be offended by a Negro teacher. Instead, he remained at Harvard in "minor fellowships" until he accepted a teaching position at West Virginia College for Negroes, where he became a one-man chemistry faculty.

Dissatisfied with the lack of facilities and stimulus at West Virginia State College, Julian left at the end of the year and went to Howard University, where he served as associate professor of chemistry for two years. At that time, in 1929, he received a Fellowship from the General Education Board and went to Vienna to study for the Ph.D. degree. There he worked under the eminent Ernst Späth, famous for his synthesis of nicotine and ephedrine. It was in Vienna that Julian became interested in the soybean, which had been imported into Germany for the manufacture of certain drugs, among them physostigmine. The structure of this drug was not known at that time, nor why it caused the pupil of the eye to contract.

Julian received the Ph.D. degree in organic chemistry[2] in 1931 and returned to Howard University, where he was appointed head of the chemistry department. He planned an extensive program of investigation into the structure and synthesis of physostigmine. Realizing that it would take many months to teach young students at Howard the techniques he had studied so carefully in Vienna, he persuaded the president of Howard to let him have the assistance of two of his Vienna colleagues who had taken their doctor's degrees with him. The three plunged into their work.

Just when their work began to show promise, a disagreement with the Howard University administration forced Julian to leave the university. When he heard about it, Dr. Blanchard, his old friend and teacher at DePauw, wired him, "Come to DePauw; I'll find you a place somewhere so that your work can go on. It must go on!" Julian went to DePauw, where he was appointed research fellow and teacher of organic chemistry. Blanchard, then dean of the

[2]Ph.D. thesis: "The Study of Certain Alkaloids and New Heterocyclic Free Radicals."

College, begged funds from the trustees, friends, and alumni, and a laboratory was fitted up.

Julian was able to bring to DePauw from Howard the ablest of his two Vienna assistants, Dr. Josef Pikl. With six students, the two began their work anew on the structure and synthesis of physostigmine. This is a drug that is powerful in the treatment of glaucoma, an eye disease. In glaucoma, the pressure inside the eyeball increases to the point where it gradually destroys the retina, resulting in blindness. Physostigmine reduces this pressure in the eye, thereby preventing blindness. The drug was known since its isolation from the seeds of the Physostigma plant (the seeds are known as Calabar beans) in 1865 by Jobst and Hesse, but no one had ever been able to synthesize or produce it artificially in the laboratory.

After considerable research, Julian presented two papers before the American Chemical Society announcing the precursors of physostigmine; that is, chemicals that lead to the formation of the physostigmine molecule. This work attracted the attention of scientists far and wide and won the acclaim of American and European scientists. This was in 1934, two years after Julian had started his work at DePauw. He was now very near his goal of actually synthesizing physostigmine in his laboratory. It was at this time that Julian's scientific work almost came to an end. DePauw did not continue to finance his research, even though it had been hailed nationally and internationally. Julian was so disillusioned that he was "almost ready to accept the early verdict of his professors that there was no future for a Negro scientist—and start making an honest living driving a truck." It was then that the Rosenwald Fund stepped in with fellowship grants to support his work for two years. These awards gave him fresh confidence and enabled him to continue his research.

Now that the financial obstacle had been overcome, a scientific obstacle appeared. Dr. Robert Robinson, the eminent head of the department of chemistry at Oxford University in England, came out with a series of publications on the synthesis of physostigmine that was entirely different from Julian's. It seemed to prove that Julian's method was wrong. His friends urged Julian to drop his physostigmine project. Dr. Robinson was too dangerous an opponent at this stage of Julian's career. But Julian was not convinced and continued with his experiments. Early in 1935, he issued a bold challenge to Dr. Robinson stating flatly that Robinson's compounds were not the precursors of physostigmine and that he, not Robinson, had the only precursors. "We shall prove the correctness of our position definitely with the final and complete synthesis of physostigmine," he wrote. Brave words!

It was at ten o'clock on a night in February, 1935, that the critical test came. After three years of work, Julian held a test tube in his hands containing pure crystals of the synthetic chemical he had built up, which he believed to be physostigmine. His assistant, Dr. Pikl, held a test tube containing natural crystals of physostigmine extracted from the Calabar bean. Identical melting points would give final proof that both were the same. Dr. Pikl began heating the tube of natural crystals at the same time as Julian began heating the tube of synthetic crystals. Dr. Blanchard, in the laboratory, watched, hardly breathing. "I'm melting!" cried Pikl. "Me too!" shouted Julian. The two thermometers registered exactly the same. It was done! The first synthesis of physostigmine had been accomplished. Then Dr. Blanchard, white man from the Deep South, and Dr. Pikl, the German colleague, and Dr. Julian, the Negro, threw their arms around one another. Their eyes were moist with happiness.

Congratulations poured in from all over Germany, from Dufraisse in France, from Hoshina in Japan and from all over America. Karrer in Switzerland published a report of the work in that year's new edition of his famous treatise on organic chemistry. The annual report of the Chemical Society of London gave a complete description of the battle. The new two-volume treatise on organic chemistry[3] by Gilman in America gave several pages to the work, including the structural formula of the newly synthesized physostigmine.[4] The *Journal of the American Chemical Society*[5] published Julian's paper dealing with the synthesis.

Dean Blanchard wanted to make Julian head of DePauw's chemistry department. He would have been the first Negro professor of chemistry in any white institution in America. However, the race prejudice that was to plague Julian again and again appeared in the form of strenuous objections from Blanchard's colleagues, who felt that the appointment was "inadvisable."

Dean Lewis of the Institute of Paper Chemistry in Appleton, Wisconsin, persuaded Julian to take

[3] H. Gilman, *Organic Chemistry* (New York: John Wiley & Sons, 1943), vol. 2, pp. 1232ff.

[4] Structural formula of physostigmine:

$$CH_3$$

COO — C — CH_2

CH_3NH — C — CH_2

N — H — N

CH_3 — CH_3

[5] Percy L. Julian and Josef Pikl, *Journal of the American Chemical Society*, vol. 57, no. 3, 1935, pp. 539, 563, 755.

a position on the research staff of the Institute. He even spent several days in Julian's laboratory talking over proposed research projects. All arrangements were made when it was suddenly discovered that an old city statute on the books of Appleton prohibited the "housing of a Negro overnight." Members of the Institute were discussing this embarrassing development one day when W. J. O'Brien, vice-president of the Glidden Company, one of the country's largest manufacturers of paints and varnishes, was present. Mr. O'Brien made a long-distance call to Julian at DePauw and offered him the post of chief chemist and director of research at Glidden. Julian accepted.

Julian's appointment at the Glidden Company is regarded as the turning point in the acceptance of Negro scientists in this country. It was the first time a Negro had the opportunity to direct a modern industrial laboratory employing a number of chemists of other races. Soon after this, other Negroes were appointed to important positions in various scientific fields. World War II, with its shortage of scientists, was another big step in providing opportunities for Negro scientists.

Julian began his work with the Glidden Company in 1936. His first task was to work out a new process for isolating and preparing commercially soybean protein to be used in the coating and sizing of paper, in cold water paints, and in textile sizing. Casein, a protein obtained from milk, had been used for coating paper but it was relatively expensive. The protein from soybeans was much cheaper and just as good. Julian's work was so successful that the Glidden Company went from a loss of $35,000 to a profit of $135,000 in just one year.

Soy protein was also used by Julian to produce a new product, "Aero-Foam," a substance that could be used to put out gasoline and oil fires by forming a "blanket" over the fire, cutting off the oxygen supply from the air. The United States Navy called it "bean soup" and used it extensively to save the lives of thousands of sailors and airmen.

While in Vienna, Julian had become interested in soybeans, which were being imported by German chemists to manufacture male and female hormones. Previously, these hormones were made from cholesterol obtained in extremely limited quantities from the brains and spinal cords of cattle. These chemists were able to extract sterols from the soybean in extremely limited quantities by a process that was very slow and costly ($100 per pound). The sterols were then converted into hormones. (Sterols are solid alcohols gotten from plants or animals.)

The major difficulty in extracting sterols from soybeans lay in the fact that the soybean oil, in

Dr. Percy L. Julian in his research laboratory at the Glidden Company

which the sterols are found, forms a hard, solid mass that prevents any chemical solvent from penetrating the oil to dissolve out the sterols. Julian noticed that the addition of quicklime to plaster of Paris made the mixture puff up into a foamy mass, completely porous. Using the same method, he converted his solid soybean oil into a porous foam through which his chemical solvents easily penetrated to remove the stubborn sterols. By this method, he began to manufacture large quantities of synthetic male and female hormones, progesterone and testosterone, from the sterols. Not only was the world supply of these hormones tremendously increased but the cost was very substantially reduced.

Among numerous uses, progesterone and testosterone have both been used effectively in the treatment of cancer. Julian's synthesis of these hormones from the common soybean ranks among the outstanding achievements of organic chemistry.

"Every problem grows into a new problem," said Julian, "and every new product lays the basis for the manufacture of another new product." About the time that the Mayo Clinic made the historic announcement of the beneficial effect of cortisone for patients with rheumatoid arthritis, Julian had been working on the synthesis of cortexolone from soybeans and had perfected a method of producing it commercially. Cortexolone, or Substance S as Julian called it, differed from cortisone by one oxygen atom. At that time, cortisone was extracted from bile, and it took the bile of 14,600 oxen to treat just one patient for one year. The cost was prohibitive. Only the rich could afford this treatment. Julian succeeded in devising a method that introduced the missing oxygen atom into his Substance S, thereby making it the equivalent of cortisone. The resulting reduction in cost from several hundred dollars per gram to a few cents per gram brought this powerful, pain-killing drug within the reach of millions of arthritis sufferers.

In 1950 Julian was honored for his work on the development of Substance S and synthetic cortisone. He was the guest of honor at a luncheon given by Mayor Kennelly and other civic leaders of Chicago. He received a tremendous ovation when the board of judges announced his name as the "Chicagoan of the Year." The entire audience rose to its feet and gave a rousing burst of applause. But the greatest thrill of all came when, to Julian's complete surprise, his parents, Mr. and Mrs. James Julian, were brought out from behind the stage curtain. In complete secrecy, the elderly Julians had been brought to Chicago from their home in Baltimore for the occasion. Many in the audience wept when the father and mother embraced their son.

In spite of this great honor, Julian had become embittered because of injustices done to the black people, and in his speech at the luncheon he said, "Friends, I appreciate deeply all this outpouring of good will, but I don't know why you should so honor me, except that I belong to a race which hangs heavily on your consciences."

Julian was to experience further instances of race hatred. Not long after the luncheon, he purchased a home in one of the most exclusive sections in suburban Oak Park near the Glidden Company in Chicago. His was the first black family in that all-white community. On Thanksgiving Day, an arsonist attempted to burn down the Julian home. Fortunately the attempt failed when neighbors summoned the firemen in time. Anger was aroused in the community and elsewhere. An editorial in the *Chicago Sun* stated:

Arsonists tried to burn down the newly purchased home of Dr. Percy Julian to keep him out of Oak Park because he is a Negro. We wonder whether these cowards whose mad prejudice drove them to commit a felony would refuse to use the lifesaving discoveries of Dr. Julian because they came from the hand and brain of a Negro. Would they refuse to take synthetic cortisone if they were wracked with the pain of arthritis? Would they forbid their wives the use of synthetic female hormone now abundantly available because of Dr. Julian's work? Would they refuse to use his synthetic physostigmine if they were afflicted with the dread eye disease, glaucoma? If they themselves were caught in a raging gasoline fire such as they tried to set, would they order the firemen not to use Dr. Julian's great discovery, chemical foam? This stuff saved the lives of thousands of American airmen and sailors after crash landings during the war. No! The bigots welcome the discoveries of Dr. Julian the scientist, but they try to exclude Dr. Julian the human being.

At a meeting of 250 clergymen, members of the Union of Ministers of Greater Chicago, a formal denunciation of the attempt to burn down Dr. Julian's home was unanimously approved. At this meeting, Sheriff John Babb said that his wife suffered from arthritis and as treatment used synthetic cortisone which Dr. Julian had synthesized from soybeans. "Does that tell you how I feel about the attempt to burn Dr. Julian's home?" he asked.

However, less than one year later, on June 12,

1951, a dynamite bomb, tossed from a speeding car, exploded under the bedroom window of the two Julian children, Faith, aged seven, and Percy, Jr., aged eleven. Their parents were away attending the funeral of Julian's father in Baltimore. Fortunately no harm came to the children. A letter to the newspaper[6] from a resident of Oak Park had scored the work of the vandals who attempted to set fire to the Julian home. When the bombing incident took place, a letter of apology, signed by forty-six neighbors, was published.[7]

[6]Chicago *Sun-Times*, November 23, 1950:

"All villagers who have been proud to live in Oak Park because they have felt it represents the finest things in American life were shocked and ashamed when they learned on Thanksgiving morning that vandals entered and attempted to burn Dr. Julian's new home. Oak Park has been proud to have as residents many eminent men and women. We should be honored that Dr. Julian, chosen as 'Chicagoan of the Year' for 1949, and Mrs. Julian, who is a scholar in her own right, planned to make their home here. This is the sort of thing that makes people outside the U.S. wonder about our democracy. We want to spread it to every country in the world. But we cannot demonstrate it in this privileged community." [Signed] Mrs. Walter E. Cowan.

[7]Chicago *Sun-Times*, July 3, 1951:

"We, as citizens of Oak Park, wish to express the dismay and indignation we feel regarding the further attack on the sanctity and security of Dr. Julian's home. We ask Dr. Julian and his family to accept our sincere apology that such un-American and bigoted action should occur in our village. We welcome them to Oak Park and are honored that they should desire to live among us. We assure them that we wish to do everything within our power to make them our real neighbors."

It was ironic that Julian was shortly thereafter approached by a real estate man in Oak Park for a favor. He had opposed Julian's buying a home there but now he was pleading with Julian to help him obtain some cortisone. Putting science above race, Julian used his influence to secure some cortisone for the man.

When, in the summer of 1951, Julian was invited to attend a national meeting of scientists at the Union League Club in Chicago, he was notified an hour before the meeting that he would not be permitted to attend. He was informed that it was against the rules of this exclusive club for a Negro to attend any functions there. Julian's answer was, "It appears to me that organizations like the Union League Club are as directly responsible as any other agency for such un-American incidents as the bombing of my home in Oak Park and the Cicero riots."

In 1954 Julian left the Glidden Company and founded his own Julian Laboratories, Inc., in Chicago and the Laboratorios Julian de Mexico in Mexico City. He specialized in the production of his Substance S, synthetic cortisone, and found that the wild yams of Mexico were even better than soybeans as a source for his products. The first year resulted in a profit of $71.70, but the net profit for the second year was $97,000. In a few years the

Julian Laboratories grew to be one of the world's largest producers of drugs processed from wild yams, cultivated in Mexico by the firm's Mexican plant and refined at the Oak Park plant. In 1961 Julian sold his Oak Park Laboratories to Smith, Kline and French, a pharmaceutical company, for the sum of $2,338,000. He remained with the firm as president at a five-figure annual salary.

Many honors and awards came to Dr. Julian. In 1947 he was awarded the Spingarn Medal; in 1949 he received the Distinguished Service Award from the Phi Beta Kappa Association; in 1950, as previously indicated, he was named "Chicagoan of the Year"; in 1951 his alma mater, DePauw University, gave him the "Old Gold Goblet" award; in 1964 he received the Honor Scroll Award from the American Institute of Chemists; in 1965, the Annual Silver Plaque Award from the National Conference of Christians and Jews; in 1967, the Founders Day Award from Loyola University in Chicago; in the same year, the Merit Award of the Chicago Technical Societies Council; and in 1968, the Chemical Pioneer Award from the American Institute of Chemists.

He was a Fellow of the American Institute of Chemists, of the Chemical Society of London, and of the New York Academy of Science. His activities included membership on the boards of trustees of Howard University, Fisk University, DePauw University, Roosevelt University, and Southern Union College. He was on the boards of directors of Chicago Theological Seminary, the NAACP Legal Defense and Educational Fund, and the Center for the Study of Democratic Institutions. He also served on the Board of Regents of the State of Illinois Colleges and Universities.

In the early 1970s, Dr. Julian was still engaged in basic research, especially in the field of sex hormones and birth control. In a conversation with the author, Dr. Julian said, "There is so much that I still have to do." How characteristic of the dedicated scientist and researcher!

Aside from his outstanding work in science, Dr. Julian was always concerned with the problems of black men and women in our society. As he once stated, "All Negroes identify with the civil rights movement because none, no matter what his income level, can escape racial discrimination." He backed Dr. Martin Luther King and the Southern Christian Leadership Conference with money. A founder of the National Negro Business and Professional Committee for the Legal Defense Fund, Dr. Julian raised funds for the NAACP Legal Defense and Educational Fund throughout the country. His son, Percy

L. Julian, Jr., a Madison, Wisconsin, lawyer whose clients included a group of antiwar demonstrators, helped to organize the Student Nonviolent Coordinating Committee (SNCC).

Dr. Julian felt that "the American ghetto and the American brand of apartheid made the Negro with genuine scientific talent and scientific yearnings probably the most poignantly tragic intellectual schizophrenic of the first half of the twentieth century." However, he was more optimistic about the future when he said, "The ghetto gloom of apartheid is slowly but surely fading on the horizon. And a completely new day is dawning for the hitherto schizophrenic Negro scientist. As he is finding his way into university faculties, where his creative talents may find uninhibited outlet, his total intellectual integrity is taking mastery over the frustrating necessity to bolster his own waning spirits. He is slowly arriving; he has faith in himself; and he is becoming a calm, determined scholar—eager, anxious, and definitely destined to write new chapters in the history of his discipline. Indeed he is doing so already! . . . The Negro scientist now need neither starve nor be condemned to a frustrating intellectual ghetto if he chooses pure science as a career." He went on to say, "It will be exciting to see the success of this new Negro intellectual in passing his experience and rebirth on to the less fortunate among his fellow men."

Dr. Julian, outstanding scientist, "soybean chemist," synthesizer of physostigmine, hormones, cortisone, and other products, and champion of civil rights for the black, was not only a credit to his race, he was a credit to the HUMAN race!

Lloyd A. Hall
1894–1971

The formation of the Institute of Food Technologists in 1939 officially confirmed the opening of a new branch of industrial chemistry by that pioneering food chemist, Dr. Lloyd A. Hall. In Hall's words, "The food technologist is a relatively new type of scientist, and people are interested in what he is and what he does to make their lives less hazardous, more enjoyable, and healthier."[1] In fact, Hall coined the slogan "More nutritious and appetizing food for longer life, through food technology." That seems to sum up the work of a food chemist.

Born in Elgin, Illinois, on June 20, 1894, Hall had an interesting family background. His maternal grandmother, who was born in Alabama, came to Illinois via the "underground railroad" at the age of

[1] L. A. Hall, "The Time Has Come," *Food Technology*, vol. 11, no. 10, 1957, pp. 8–16.

Dr. Lloyd A. Hall, pioneer in food chemistry

sixteen. His paternal grandfather (a free Negro) came to Chicago in 1837 and was one of the founders of the Quinn Chapel A. M. E. Church and its first pastor in 1841. This is the first and oldest colored church in Chicago. His parents, Augustus and Isabel Hall, were both high school graduates.

Young Hall attended the East Side High School in Aurora, Illinois, where his interest in chemistry began. In Hall's words, "I became interested in chemistry while attending high school, where I registered for a Science course. Chemistry was not well known when I began my high school studies in 1908 and not many students were interested in the sciences at that time, but all types of sciences were of great concern to me and I graduated among the top ten in my class of one hundred and twenty-five. During the four years in high school there were only five Negro-American students—four girls and one boy (this was me). I also participated in debating and athletics—Captain of the Debating Team for one year and a letter man on the track team and baseball team, and a sub on the football team. I still had the time and initiative to deliver morning newspapers. Four scholarships were given to me to attend outstanding Illinois universities on graduation. I chose Northwestern University."[2]

At Northwestern, Hall worked his way through college and majored in chemistry. There he met a fellow student, Carroll L. Griffith, who was assigned

[2]Communication from Dr. Hall to the author, dated May 7, 1969.

to the same bench in one of the chemistry laboratories at the college. Later he was to spend some thirty-four years in the Griffith Laboratories doing his most important work in food chemistry. In 1916 he graduated with a B.S. degree. He went on to do graduate work at the University of Chicago in chemistry.

When Hall looked for a job, he encountered discrimination. He had been hired by telephone by the Western Electric Company. When he reported for work, however, they looked at him and then told him that there was no work for him. Shaken by the rejection, but still hoping that a mistake had been made, he telephoned the personnel office again and met the shouted reply, "We don't take niggers!"

Fortunately, in 1916, his chemistry background secured him a position as chemist in the Chicago Department of Health Laboratories, where, one year later, he rose to the position of senior chemist. Two years later he left to become chief chemist for the John Morrell Company in Ottumwa, Iowa, where he remained for two years.

On September 23, 1919, Hall married Myrrhene E. Newsome, a graduate of the Western State College for teachers in Macomb, Illinois. Two years after his marriage he moved to a larger company, the Boyer Chemical Laboratory in Chicago, where he served as chief chemist. By this time, Hall's interest had turned to the chemistry of foods, a new field of chemistry, and in 1922 he became president and chemical director of a consulting laboratory— the Chemical Products Corporation, in Chicago. After using his services as a consultant, the Griffith Laboratories asked him to come to work for them full time. Hall accepted and in 1925 was appointed chief chemist and director of research, a position he maintained until his retirement in 1959.

Before Hall went to the Griffith Laboratories, salts for curing and preserving foods were not very satisfactory and very little was known about them. Since ancient times, sodium chloride (common table salt) has been used as a meat preservative. Long ago it became known that nitrogen-containing chemicals like sodium nitrate or potassium nitrate, in addition to sodium chloride, were beneficial. In particular, the mixture reddened the meat, and its color and appearance were better. Then it became known that nitrate alone improved the color and appearance of meat. The effectiveness of the nitrate was due to nitrate being chemically changed into nitrite (one oxygen atom less than the nitrate) and the nitrite into nitrous acid, which produces a red color by chemical union with the hemoglobin in meat.

Hall found that when a mixture of sodium chlo-

ride, sodium nitrate, and sodium nitrite *ᵘ*
to preserve and cure meat, the sodium chl/
etrated the meat slowly, the nitrate faste.,
nitrite much faster. This was not desirable, since
the faster penetration of the nitrate and nitrite caused
the meat to disintegrate before the sodium chloride
could penetrate to preserve it. Something had to be
done to prevent the nitrate and nitrite from acting
before the sodium chloride had its chance to penetrate. Hall solved this problem by the ingenious
method of enclosing the nitrate and nitrite *inside*
the sodium chloride crystal. This he did by "flash
drying" the solution of these salts.

In the process of flash drying, Hall took a strong
solution of sodium chloride containing small amounts
of the nitrogen-containing salts (nitrate and nitrite).
He dried the solution quickly by evaporating it over
heated metal rollers. The resulting crystals had the
characteristic cubic form of sodium chloride crystals, but under the microscope one could see the
nitrogen-containing salts inside the heartlike center
of the crystal. In this way, the sodium chloride could
dissolve and penetrate to preserve the meat before
the nitrogen-containing nitrates and nitrites, inside
the salt crystals, could be released to cure the meat.

Hall's flash dried crystals were far superior to
any meat-curing salts ever produced and were widely

ped in the meat industry. However, another problem arose in connection with their storage. When stored in drums or other containers, the salt mixture tended to absorb moisture from the air and cake (form a solid mass) on standing. This was a serious hindrance to its use. Hall went back to the laboratory. He tried out various hygroscopic agents, that is, chemicals that absorb moisture from the air. By adding such chemicals to the salt mixture, these chemicals, instead of the salt mixture itself, would absorb the moisture. Improvement was noted, but caking was not entirely prevented. From his experimentation, Hall finally discovered that a combination of glycerine (hygroscopic agent) and another chemical, alkali metal tartrate, gave the best results. When this tartrate and glycerine were present in the salt solution to be flash dried, the resulting crystals were more powdery in character and flowed like water. No more caking took place and once more Hall had solved the problem. Softening the hard water before flash drying also helped greatly.

Another area that occupied much of Hall's research was the sterilization of foods and substances associated with food. Many people are under the impression that spices are used to preserve foods. Hall found, to the contrary, that many spices marketed carried with them millions of germs in the form of bacteria, molds, and yeasts. Natural spices such as cloves, cinnamon, ginger, paprika, allspice, sage, and others are a type of food ingredient used in small amounts, yet usually infested with spores of molds, yeasts, and bacteria. Even dried vegetables (onion powder and garlic powder) were guilty of contaminating food. Meat packers adding spices to their meat products were actually contaminating these products.

Hall undertook long and exhaustive research and experimentation in this new area. How could he effectively sterilize these foodstuffs and at the same time preserve their appearance, quality, and flavor with no noticeable change? Spices and dried vegetables became darkened by being heated in air. They lost their flavor and aroma when exposed to evaporation or oxidation. Sterilizing spices by dry or moist heat above 240°F ruined the color and flavor of the spices so as to make them unmarketable.

After experimenting with a number of chemicals, Hall hit upon the chemical ethylene oxide, a gas. The ability of ethylene oxide to kill insects was well known. Hall now used it to kill germs in foodstuffs. First, however, the chemical had to penetrate the food in order to reach the germs. This was difficult because of the moisture and gases that covered the surface and interior of the substances to be sterilized, preventing the entrance of the germ-killing ethylene oxide gas. Hall solved this problem by first subjecting the foodstuff to a vacuum. This removed moisture and cleaned the surfaces and interior of the food of gases. In this way, the foodstuff was activated to take up the sterilizing gas. He then introduced ethylene oxide gas into the vacuum chamber for a period of time necessary to sterilize the material. Conditions of time and temperature differed for different bacteria, molds, and yeasts.

The introduction of sterilized spices to the meat-packing industry did much to revolutionize that industry. This process was also applied to drugs, medicines, medical supplies, cosmetic materials, dentrifices, and so on. Sterilization with ethylene oxide has become a very large business in the United States on hospital supplies such as bandages, dressings, and sutures. Hall's method is in general use throughout the country.

There was another big problem in food chemistry that Hall now attacked. Fats and oils often became "spoiled" or rancid and therefore unfit for human consumption. Some of the constituents of fats and oils are known to possess the tendency to react with the oxygen in the air. Rancidity develops primarily from the products formed during this oxidation. These products impart an undesirable odor and taste. Chemicals called antioxidants retard or prevent this oxidation and thereby the development of rancidity in fats and oils and foods containing them. It was with these antioxidants that Hall now worked.

He experimented with many different kinds of antioxidants. He found that crude (not refined) vegetable oils contained the tocopherols that acted as antioxidants. His experiments showed that such chemicals as lecithin, propyl gallate, and ascorbyl palmitate were also excellent antioxidants. But there was difficulty in mixing the antioxidant properly with the food to be protected against rancidity. Propyl gallate, for example, was almost insoluble in fat and therefore would not mix with the food to be protected. Hall solved this problem by using lecithin as a "carrier." The propyl gallate would dissolve in the lecithin and then this solution would be introduced into the fatty food (lard, for example). Later on, he substituted citric acid for the lecithin and produced an antioxidant salt mixture made up of:

Propyl gallate	0.101%
Citric acid	0.094%
Propylene glycol	0.165%
Salt (sodium chloride) . .	99.640%

Now, with the addition of this antioxidant salt mixture, foods containing fats or oils could be protected against spoilage or rancidity. These antioxidants are in very wide use today in the food industry.

In 1951, Hall and an associate patented a process for curing bacon which reduced the time of curing—usually six to fifteen days—to a matter of hours. The products were more uniform and had better stability and a better appearance.

Another field where Hall devoted much time was protein hydrolysates. Proteins are said to be hydrolyzed when they are broken down into simpler compounds either in the laboratory or in the human body. The products of this hydrolysis, or breaking down, are called hydrolysates. Hall's hydrolysates were flavoring materials used in foods that he derived from the hydrolysis of various proteins. Griffith Laboratories has substantial manufacturing facilities for protein hydrolysates and Hall was again a pioneer in this field.

Hall had many other interests, which included the fields of seasoning, spice extractives, and enzymes. He spent a considerable time in consulting work which led to a variety of projects such as puncture-sealing compositions. He had a very active interest in detergents, vitamins, and asphalt. He devoted substantial time to the development of yeast foods. These different fields led to the issuance of an additional twenty-six patents. By 1970, Hall had been granted approximately 105 United States and foreign patents on products and methods he invented. He was the author of about fifty scientific papers.

In two wars, Hall served as science adviser. In World War I he was Assistant Chief Inspector of Powder and Explosives in the Ordnance Department of the U.S. Army from 1917 to 1919. In World War II, he was a member of the Committee on Food Research of the Scientific Advisory Board, Quartermaster Corps, War Department, from 1943 to 1948. There he was invaluable in solving problems of maintaining military food supplies in pure and palatable form.

In addition to his work, Hall found time to serve on the Illinois State Food Commission of the State Department of Agriculture (1944–49); as a consultant to the George W. Carver Foundation (1946–48); as a consultant to the Food and Agricultural Organization of the United Nations, in which capacity he spent six months in Indonesia (1961); as a member of the Executive Board of the Institute of Food Technologists (1951–55); and as a member of the Food Technology Council of the Illinois Institute of Technology (1948–55). He was a charter member of the Institute of Food Technologists (1939) and the editor of its magazine, *The Vitalizer* (1948), as well as on its Executive Board (1951–55).

Hall was very active in the American Institute of Chemists. In 1954 he became chairman of the Chicago chapter and the following year a member of the national board of directors. He served on the Institute's committee on professional education. When he was elected councilor-at-large and member of the board of directors, he thereby became the first black man to hold that office in the Institute's thirty-two-year history. In 1956 he was awarded the Honor Scroll of the Chicago chapter "because of his intense interest and influence in promoting professional attitudes and constructive actions in the profession of chemistry, and for his numerous achievements in the field of food chemistry." Again, in 1959, Hall received the honorary membership award from the Institute for "noteworthy leadership in food and biological chemistry."

Besides Fellowship in the American Institute of Chemists, Hall was also a Fellow of the American Association for the Advancement of Science, the American Public Health Association, and the New York Academy of Sciences. His other honors included Phi Tau Sigma (honorary food science fraternity), Sigma Xi (honorary scientific fraternity),

Brotherhood Award from the Chicago Conference on Brotherhood (1957), Honor Award from the Chicago Committee of 100 (1957), and Certificate of Appreciation from the Quartermaster Corps for services in World War II. He was listed in *American Men of Science*, *Who's Who in Chemistry*, *Who's Who in Colored America*, and *Who's Who in America*.

He was a member of the Chicago Executive Committee of the National Association for the Advancement of Colored People (1932–34) and on the Board of Directors of the Chicago Urban League (1935–36). From 1956 to 1959 he was a member of the Hyde Park–Kenwood Conservation Community Council, the first urban renewal project in Chicago. As a member of the Board of Trustees of the Chicago Planetarium Society (1959–60) he served as education and science adviser to the Adler Planetarium. From 1962 to 1964 he was a member of the American Food for Peace Council, appointed by President Kennedy.

In 1959 Hall retired from the Griffith Laboratories and moved to Pasadena, California. He left because of his wife's health and the necessity to live in a warmer climate. Needless to say, he continued his civic and scientific work in California.

Hall did not separate the chemist from the citizen. He claimed that scientists in the past had been reluctant to take time to tell the public who they were, what they thought, and what they did. It's not that the scientists are different from others. Only now scientists are arriving at the point where they want themselves and their work understood by the public at large. They want professional status and public acceptance, not only as scientists but as active citizens as well.

Ernest Everett Just
1883–1941

With five dollars in his pocket and an extra pair of
shoes in his hand, the young lad of seventeen stepped
off the boat at New York City. Tall and slender, his
fine, sensitive features glowing with eagerness and
anticipation, he had come all the way from Charleston, South Carolina, working his way on this small
ship. He had heard of the Kimball Academy in
Meriden, New Hampshire, and was determined to
make enough money in New York to be able to enter
the Academy as a student. This determined lad was
Ernest E. Just.

Born in Charleston, South Carolina, on August
14, 1883, Just received his elementary schooling at
a public school for black children—the Industrial
School of Orangeburg. His father, a dock builder in
Charleston, died when the boy was four years old.
His mother taught school in order to support the
family. Young Just helped out by working in the

Ernest Everett Just, outstanding marine biologist

fields after school. Schools for blacks in the South were so inferior that after he finished his elementary school, Just and his mother decided it was best for him to go North for his further education.

Once in New York City, he worked feverishly

and long, and in four weeks he had earned enough money to go to New Hampshire and the Kimball Academy. As a student at Kimball, he had a brilliant record. He was editor of the school paper and president of its debating society. He did the four years at the Academy in three years, with honors. In 1903 he graduated and entered Dartmouth College in New Hampshire.

It was at Dartmouth that Just was inspired to enter the field of study that was to occupy the rest of his life. He studied under a famous zoologist, William Patten. In his first course in biology he read an essay on the development of the egg cell and was so profoundly influenced by it that he took all the courses in biology offered by the college. In his senior year he devoted a good deal of time to a research problem. When he received his A.B. degree in 1907, he was elected to the Phi Beta Kappa honorary fraternity, with special honors in zoology and history. He was the only *magna cum laude* in his class.

Three months after graduation, in October, 1907, Just went to Howard University to teach, at a salary of four hundred dollars a year. Howard, at that time, was mainly an undergraduate school with very few facilities for postgraduate study. Although he continued his work on the development of the egg cell, practically all his research was done at the Marine Biological Laboratories in Woods Hole, Massachusetts, where, beginning in 1912, he was to spend every summer but two. It was said that he spent his life teaching in winter and doing research in the summer. Just was the type of man who needed for his growth a large university with its well-equipped laboratories and opportunities for creative work. Otherwise it was like putting an eagle in a chicken coop.

Just began his graduate training at Woods Hole in 1909 with a course in marine invertebrates and in 1910 in embryology. In the summers of 1911 and 1912 he acted as research assistant to Dr. Frank R. Lillie, head of the department of zoology at the University of Chicago, where Just was later to do his doctoral work. The subject of their research was fertilization and breeding habits in the Nereis (sandworm) and in the sea urchin. These experiences focused Just's interest on marine eggs, which remained the center of his investigations throughout life.

His duties at Howard University delayed the completion of his work for the doctor's degree (Ph.D.) at the University of Chicago until 1916. In the meantime, he completed six papers, based on work at Woods Hole. His work was so good, and his efforts during the academic year to improve medical education at Howard and other black institutions so effective, that in 1915 he received the first award of the Spingarn Medal. The award was presented by Charles S. Whitman, governor of the State of New York. By this time, Howard students had been acclaiming him through their newspapers for several years. Throughout his long career, he held the esteem of one generation of Howard students after another. He was Howard's vindication before the scientific world. In 1923 *The Howard Bison* (student annual) was dedicated to him "whose exemplary scholarship has been a source of inspiration to all of us."

His first paper (1912) was an interesting study in which he showed by an ingenious method that the point of entrance of the spermatozoon in the egg of the Nereis determined the way in which the egg would develop. This was followed by more than sixty papers in the next twenty-five years dealing with fertilization and experimental parthenogenesis (development of an egg without fertilization) in marine eggs. His work in parthenogenesis corrected some of the earlier work done by the eminent Jacques Loeb in that area.

Just's period of study and investigation at Woods Hole took place during the greatest decade in the history of this laboratory. He came in contact with and was influenced by some of the world's leading scientists. It was during this time that some of America's most significant biological contributions were made at Woods Hole. Lillie's work in fertilization, Loeb's work in parthenogenesis and regeneration, Newman's work in twinning and genetics, and Carlson's work in physiology were some of the contributions during the time in which Just was associated with the Marine Biological Laboratories.

In the twenty summer sessions that Just spent at Woods Hole, he became the foremost authority in the embryological resources of the marine group of animals. He learned to handle the material with skill and understanding, and as a result, was in great demand, especially by physiologists, who often knew their physics and chemistry better than their biology. They came to him for advice and assistance, which he gave generously.

Just's curiosity concentrated upon the cell, the primary unit of life. Every living thing is made up of cells. For a long time, biologists felt that the nucleus of the cell controlled and dominated all the activities of the cell. The cytoplasm (protoplasm or living substance in a cell outside of the nucleus) was considered relatively unimportant and hardly anyone ever mentioned the ectoplasm, the outer surface of the cytoplasm. Early in Just's research, this ectoplasm began to take on great significance for him. After twenty-five years of research, observing minutely, under the microscope, the egg cells of marine animals, he declared most emphatically that the ectoplasm was just as important as the nucleus, that the cell as a living unit depended on the smooth cooperation between the nucleus and the cytoplasm, and that because of its closer relationship to the outside environment, the ectoplasm was primarily responsible for whatever individuality and harmonious development the cell had.

All this was contrary to beliefs popularly held by most biologists at that time and Just's research findings changed scientific opinion concerning the very roots of life. They made scientists reconsider many ideas formerly held. Prominent textbooks on the cell incorporated Just's findings in later editions of their texts. These findings affected scientists' thinking on such fundamental things as the real difference between living and nonliving things, the way to determine sex in advance, the key to evolution, and the difference between plant and animal life. They also had a great bearing on medicine through a new understanding of the functions of the liver, the kidneys, the pancreas, and other vital organs from the standpoint of a new relationship between the cell and its surroundings, through the ectoplasm. The bearing of these research findings on the fight against cancer was pointed out by some scientists.

Just dismissed the gene theory of heredity as an "ultra-mechanistic, rigidly bound concept." He denied the almost magical power ascribed to the gene in determining hereditary characteristics. While he did not deny that the gene played a role in heredity, he claimed that the hereditary factors were located in the cytoplasm and that the genes merely functioned in extracting materials containing these hereditary factors from the cytoplasm. "Only in as much as they take out substances from the cytoplasm do the genes determine heredity," he said.

Reducing the nucleus to relatively minor significance, Just gave greatest importance, as far as growth and evolution were concerned, to the ectoplasm. Its importance began with fertilization (union of sperm and egg cells), on which Just had made many studies. His research proved that fertilization of the egg cell depended on conditions of the cytoplasm independent of the state of the nucleus in the egg cell. He showed that fertilization was primarily a reaction between the egg, the ectoplasm of the egg, and the spermatozoon. His experiments and researches into fertilization proved that the ecto-plasm was necessary for fertilization to take place at all; that the success or failure of fertilization to take place was correlated with the appearance and disappearance of an ectoplasm substance; that fer-tilization depended on the integrity of the layer of ectoplasm; and finally, that polyspermy (the en-trance into the egg cell of more than one sperma-tozoon) takes place when the ectoplasm is slow in reacting.

Regarding the surface of the cell as something much more than the "semi-permeable membrane" of the physiologists, Just conceived the behavior of the ectoplasm as one prime factor in the develop-ment of the egg, the other being the building up of nuclear material. He maintained that there was con-stant interplay of both with the protoplasm in gen-eral. "As the boundary, the living mobile limit of the cell, the ectoplasm controls the integration be-tween the living cell and all else external to it. It is keyed to the outside world as no other part of the cell. It stands guard over the peculiar form of the living substance and is a buffer against the attacks of the surroundings and the means of communication with it."

In 1912, two important events took place in

Just's life. He married Ethel Highwarden, a teacher in a high school in Washington, and he was elevated to a full professorship and head of the department of zoology at Howard University with his salary raised to $1200 a year. Three years later, he took a leave of absence from Howard to complete his doctoral studies at the University of Chicago under Dr. Frank R. Lillie, head of the zoology department and the man he worked under at Woods Hole. In 1916 he received the Ph.D. degree in zoology. He then returned to Howard and to his summers at Woods Hole.

Just became a member of the Corporation of the Marine Biological Laboratory at Woods Hole and associate editor of the *Biological Bulletin*, the *Journal of Morphology*, *Physiological Zoology*, and *Protoplasma* of Berlin. He was contributing editor to *General Cytology* and to a work in colloid chemistry by Jerome Alexander (1928). He was the author of more than sixty publications in scientific journals.

An element of tragedy ran through all of Just's scientific career because of the limitations imposed by being a black man in America. Just was respected and honored outside this country, and it is partly because of the lack of recognition here that he spent his last few years in self-imposed exile. The great

Russian biologist, Koltzov, begged him to remain in Russia, where he would have been received on an honored basis. In 1929, Just received an invitation from Dr. M. Hartmann, of the Kaiser Wilhelm Institute for Biology, to be a guest worker in his institution. This was a signal honor since the Institute at that time was one of the greatest research laboratories in the world in physics, chemistry, and biology. Numbered among its members were Nobel Prize winners. Just spent seven months at the Institute in research. He was also welcomed and conducted research at the Sorbonne in Paris, France, and at the Naples Zoological Station in Italy. The many fellowships and research awards show the high esteem in which he was held as a scientist, but they did not compensate for his failure to receive an appointment in one of the large American universities or research institutes.

Speaking of Just in a 1969 publication, Dr. Percy L. Julian, the famous black chemist, said, "Just's beautiful papers, dealing mostly with artificial parthenogenesis, represented the first respectable scientific contributions from the pen of a Negro as the senior author. Going back to the ghetto to teach, after securing his doctor's degree, he suffered the nine months isolation of the school year until the surcease of a summer's retreat at the Woods Hole Marine Biology Center gave him the opportunity to bury himself in creditable investigations."[1]

Dr. E. P. Lyons, Dean of the University of Minnesota Medical School, stated, "The greatest problem in American biology is Professor Just. He properly belongs to an institution like the Rockefeller Institute, and he was the most logical candidate to take the place of Jacques Loeb when he died, but the Rockefeller Foundation, spending millions of dollars to combat disease internationally, could not summon enough courage to solve an interracial problem. By its example it could have set a precedent to follow that science knows no race nor creed. What it actually did was only catering to old prejudices in spite of its presumed internationalism."

In addition to his voluminous writings, in 1939 Just published two books. The first was an account of the very refined methods and techniques that he had developed for work in the field of experimentation with the eggs of marine animals,[2] and it was eagerly awaited by biologists researching that area.

[1]Stanton L. Wormley, and L. H. Fenderson (editors), *Many Shades of Black* (New York: William Morrow & Company, 1969). (Chapter by P. L. Julian.)

[2]E. E. Just, *Basic Methods for Experiments in Eggs of Marine Animals* (Philadelphia: P. Blakiston & Company, 1939).

The second book, the more important one, summarized his life's work in the fundamental field of cell physiology.[3] In this book, Just showed that the concept of the absolute independence of the germ cells from the rest of the body was false. He insisted on the interdependence and interaction of the cytoplasm and the nucleus of the cell, and he emphasized the significance of the environment. "The most potent objection to the gene concept as the unit of life," said Just, "lies in the fact that the gene theory fails to explain how a single cell, the egg, becomes a complex animal. The living thing is part of the natural world; it grows and lives on the stuff of which it is made and whence it comes. Then living things and outside world constitute one interdependent unit, as evolution teaches and as the development of an animal egg reveals."

The book demonstrates the thesis, to which Just devoted a lifetime, that the cell nucleus is not the sole structure that is responsible for heredity, but that the cytoplasm and especially the ectoplasm influence the structure and function of the nucleus so greatly as to share equal responsibility. By so doing, he directed the attention of biologists to a most neglected field of research—the cytoplasm

[3] E. E. Just, *The Biology of the Cell Surface* (Philadelphia: P. Blakiston & Sons, 1939).

and ectoplasm of the cell and the influence of external environment on these.

When he withdrew from Woods Hole to work in European laboratories, his loss to the scientific community at Woods Hole was deeply felt. That Just appreciated Dr. Lillie's contribution to his development is shown by the fact that he cut short a study in Naples, Italy, in order to return to Woods Hole in 1930 to participate in a special seminar commemorating Dr. Lillie's sixtieth birthday and fortieth anniversary as a worker at Woods Hole.

Two years after the publication of his life's work, Just succumbed to cancer. He died on October 27, 1941, at the age of fifty-eight. Besides his wife, Mrs. Ethel H. Just, he was survived by two daughters, Margaret and Maribel, and a son, Highwarden Just.

In an obituary, Just's white friend, teacher, and collaborator, Dr. Frank R. Lillie, said, "His death was premature and his work unfinished; but his accomplishments were many and worthy of remembrance. That a man of his ability, scientific devotion, and of such strong personal loyalties as he gave and received should have been warped in the land of his birth must remain a matter for regret."

Pioneer in the field of zoology, outstanding scientist and teacher, Spingarn Medal winner, authority in the field of marine biology, Just was first and foremost a student of the meaning of life. The branch of science called biology was his field, but his effort to put the finger on life, what it is made of, how it begins, where it is going, went much deeper than any branch of science.

What opportunities American science has missed by failing to provide Just with the opportunities that he was entitled to! His contributions were not to blacks, or Americans, but to the better understanding and enhancement of life for all peoples everywhere, and indeed for all living things.

Daniel Hale Williams
1856–1931

"Sewed Up His Heart" shouted the headline of the
Chicago *Daily Inter-Ocean*. History had just been
made. In a time when few surgeons dared to operate
on the abdomen, let alone on the heart, Dr. Williams
had successfully operated on a dying man who had
been stabbed in the heart. The man not only survived but he lived for fifty years afterward. It was
the first time in the history of medicine that this
kind of surgery was attempted, and it was performed
successfully! What was the background of this great
pioneering surgeon?

Born in Hollidaysburg, Pennsylvania, on January 18, 1856, Dan was the fifth of a family of seven
children. His father, of mixed Negro and white an-
cestry, had learned the practice of barbering from
his father. Very active in the Abolitionist cause, he
was a prominent member of the Equal Rights League.

Daniel Hale Williams, pioneer in surgery

His mother's family included Negro, white, and Indian ancestors.

At the age of forty-seven Dan's father died of consumption, leaving his wife and seven children in financial difficulties. Dan, who was ten years old at the time, was apprenticed to a shoemaker in Baltimore, and his mother left Pennsylvania and went to Rockford, Illinois. Unhappy with his lot, Dan managed to run away and rejoin his mother in Illinois. A few months later, however, his mother returned east without him. Left on his own, Dan worked on lake steamers and learned the barber's trade. When his oldest sister, Sally, wrote asking him to join her in Edgerton, Wisconsin, Dan jumped at the chance. Opportunities for the Negro were greater in the West than in the South and he soon opened his own barbershop in Edgerton at the age of seventeen. But Janesville, a few miles away, had schools, an opera house, and flourishing industries, so Sally and Dan moved there, and Dan got a job in the barbershop of Harry Anderson. After Dan's sister married and left Janesville, Anderson took Dan into his home and treated him as one of the family.

Dan began to attend Haire's Classical Academy, which was the equivalent of the present high school. After graduating, he clerked and read the law in a lawyer's office for about one year, no doubt influenced by his older brother, who was already a successful practicing lawyer. However, he soon realized that the law was not for him.

In Janesville everybody stood in awe of Dr. Henry Palmer, a local physician. Dr. Palmer was an excellent surgeon who had been the director of the largest military hospital during the Civil War and surgeon general of Wisconsin for ten years. News of Dr. Palmer's exciting work was often in the local newspaper, and when Dan read of it, he was determined that medicine was going to be his life's work. At the age of twenty-two he became an apprentice in Dr. Palmer's office. He stayed there for two years reading medicine, learning to practice, and scrubbing up the office at the end of the day.

In those days it was customary for a person to open his own private practice of medicine at the end of two years of apprenticeship in a doctor's office. Few physicians at that time had gone to medical college. Dan, however, under Dr. Palmer's influence, was determined to obtain the best medical training available. In 1880, with a one-hundred-dollar bank loan in his pocket, Dan went off to Chicago Medical College (later to become Northwestern University Medical School). At that time, Chicago Medical College was one of the best medical schools in the country and had the "heroically high standard" of an eighteen-months' course. Although standards were very high, laboratory work was virtually nonexistent, and the staff lectured, and operated also, in stiff collars and black swallow-tails. Dan graduated from medical school in 1883 and opened an office at Thirty-first Street and Michigan Avenue in Chicago.

Dan Williams' true place in medicine must be measured against the background of his times. A new era in surgery began in the eighties. As a graduate in 1883, he belonged to a group of young men not bound by the prejudices of the previous generation and receptive to new thoughts and practices in surgery. A revolution was taking place in this field because of the work of Louis Pasteur in France and Joseph Lister in England. In the late seventies, Pasteur had laid the foundations of bacteriology. He had proven the relationship between certain microorganisms and specific diseases. He set forth his "Germ Theory of Disease" that was to sweep the medical world. Lister applied Pasteur's theory and revolutionized surgery by demonstrating the effectiveness of antiseptics (germ-killing chemicals) in the treatment of wounds. A furor was created, although it was difficult for the doctrine of antisepsis to gain acceptance among the older men of that day.

Many explanations of disease were offered before Pasteur. It was thought that illness was caused by demons inhabiting the body. The art of healing was dominated by superstition, witchcraft, and misinformation. Surgery was practiced by barbers. It was held that a sick person was filled with bad blood and for a cure should be bled. In many cases, patients who should have been given blood had blood taken from them instead. More patients died from the treatment than from the disease.

It remained for Pasteur to prove that disease was caused by harmful microorganisms or germs within the body. His work was to result in the virtual elimination of many diseases caused by germs. This knowledge was just beginning to be known in Williams' day. Abdominal and chest surgery was rarely if ever attempted, because even if successful the infection that invariably followed caused the death of the patient.

Ether was given as an anesthetic to a human being for the first time in 1842, during an operation by Dr. Long of Georgia. Today we have a choice of many anesthetics, both general and local. We also have sulfa drugs and antibiotics to help fight infection.

When Williams began to practice medicine, Pasteur's germ theory of disease, Lister's antiseptic surgery, and the availability of anesthetics opened new vistas for the surgeon, and Williams was in a position to take advantage of these "new" advances. Operations could be attempted now that were previously out of the question.

In his practice of medicine, "Dr. Dan," as his patients and friends came to call him, turned more and more to surgery. In those days operations in private homes were common. Not only did people distrust hospitals but Negroes could not gain admission except in the city's charity wards, where they were either neglected or used for experimentation. Furthermore, Negro doctors could not get hospital appointments because of racial prejudice, and therefore could not get their patients into hospitals. It was also impossible for Negro women to get training as nurses since training schools would not accept them.

Williams' first operation took place in Mrs. LeBeau's dining room, where he removed her hemorrhoids. He went on to do more and more surgery in the kitchens and dining rooms of patients' homes. In each case he applied Lister's principles of antiseptic surgery conscientiously and meticulously. He scrubbed the entire room with soap and water. He then sprayed carbolic acid, a strong germ killer, all over the room and followed that by sterilizing all the instruments to be used in the operation in a wash boiler filled with steam. Hands and clothing were also included in the cleaning and sterilizing process. His results were excellent. Infection, the feared and dangerous aftermath of surgery, was avoided.

Soon Dr. Dan's reputation as a successful surgeon spread and he was appointed to the surgical staff of the South Side Dispensary in Chicago. He also became clinical instructor and demonstrator in anatomy at the Chicago Medical College, where one of his students was Charlie Mayo of the famous Mayo Brothers. Later still he became surgeon to the City Railway Company, a position never previously held by a Negro physician. His appointment to the Illinois State Board of Health in 1889 was indicative of the kind of recognition he was shown. While the position carried no salary, it carried tremendous prestige.

In describing Williams' surgical skill, Dr. U. G. Dailey, a former student of his, said, "His surgical work was marked by profound anatomical knowledge, a thorough understanding of physiology—normal and pathological—and an uncanny surgical judgment. As an operator, his attention to technical detail was meticulous."

It was a cold, wintry day in 1890. Dr. Dan was sitting in the warm, comfortable parlor of his friend, the Reverend Louis Reynolds, pastor of St.

Stephen's African Methodist Church. The Reverend Reynolds had just asked him to use his influence to have Reynolds' sister admitted to a training course for nurses in one of the Chicago hospitals normally closed to Negro applicants. Williams thought for a moment and then said, "No. I don't think I'll try to get your sister into one of these training courses. We'll do something better. We'll start a hospital of our own and we'll train dozens and dozens of nurses." He went on, "There must be a hospital for Negroes but not a Negro hospital." Williams had been thinking of it for some time. He was well established in private practice by 1890 and was famed for his surgical skill, but still as a Negro he lacked a hospital appointment. This lack, and his indignation that all Negro patients were thrown into the city's charity wards, made him determined to start a new kind of hospital—one to be owned, staffed, and managed by blacks and whites together. Here Negro sick and poor would receive the best of care, ambitious young Negro doctors would have their chance, and young black women, not admitted to white schools, would be trained for the nursing the times demanded.

Williams threw himself into this new effort with enthusiasm. He formed committees of black and white people. He spoke at churches, street corners, club meetings, and anywhere else he was permitted to speak. He got the cooperation of many people, rich and poor, black and white. The idea of a hospital run by Negroes where Negroes would be received on an equal basis was very appealing to the black community.

On January 23, 1891, medical history was made. The first interracial hospital in the United States was founded. Articles of incorporation were drawn up in the name of the Provident Hospital and Training School Association. The trustees, executive committee, and finance committee were all colored. The hospital itself opened its doors in May 1891— a three-story building at Twenty-ninth Street and Dearborn, with room for twelve beds. The first year, out of 175 applicants for nurse training, Dr. Dan accepted seven, the sister of the Reverend Reynolds among them. All were high school graduates. The training period was for eighteen months.

The staff of Provident Hospital was made up of Negro and white doctors carefully selected for their qualifications. George Hall was one of the Negro doctors whose application was rejected by Dr. Dan. Hall's medical training was very poor and his medical diploma came from the Eclectic School in Chicago, a dubious institution. Hall accused Williams of discrimination and succeeded in convincing the trustees to appoint him to the staff. He was given an unimportant appointment in the children's clinic. From that time Hall became the lifelong enemy of Williams and sought to discredit him whenever he could.

At the end of the first year, of 189 sick and injured treated at the Provident Hospital, twenty-three had improved, three had not, twenty-two had died, and 141 recovered entirely—a remarkable record when only desperate cases were taken to a hospital. However, the economic depression of 1893 began to threaten Provident's existence. At that time help came in the form of Frederick Douglass, one of the most important Negro leaders in the country. It was the year of the Chicago World's Fair and Douglass came as the Haitian commissioner. At the Fair he urged Negroes to contribute to Provident Hospital, the type of interracial organization of which he highly approved. Money began to come in and things became easier for the hospital after the Fair.

July 9, 1893, was a hot and humid day in Chicago and tempers were short. A fight in a saloon ended in the stabbing of a young Negro expressman, James Cornish. He was rushed to Provident Hospital with a one-inch knife wound in the chest near the heart. The call went out for Dr. Dan. By the time he arrived Cornish had collapsed from loss of blood and shock and it was obvious that he would soon die if nothing was done. But what could be done? Opening the chest cavity in those days was an invitation to death. Nobody would have criticized Williams if he had followed the standard treatment in this case of "absolute rest, cold, and opium" after which the patient invariably died. Why should he risk his surgical reputation? If he did not operate and the patient died, nobody would blame him. If he did operate and the patient died, he would be condemned by the medical profession. X rays had not as yet been discovered to help him, blood transfusions were unknown at that time, sulfa drugs and antibiotics to fight infection were also unknown. What to do? The patient was sinking. Dr. Dan decided to operate.

Six physicians—four white and two black—witnessed the operation. Dr. Dan worked swiftly. He opened the chest cavity and saw that the knife used in the stabbing had penetrated the heart about one-tenth of an inch, and had cut the pericardium (the sac surrounding the heart) one and one-quarter inches in length. He decided that the heart muscle did not need any suturing (sewing up), but he did suture the pericardium. The atmosphere was tense as he worked and continued to be so until he finally closed up the wound. It was a daring operation—the first time a surgeon had entered the chest cavity. Would it work? Would the dread infection set in and kill the patient? On August 30, fifty-one days after Cornish had entered the hospital a dying man, he was discharged completely recovered. He lived for fifty years afterward and died in 1943, having outlived his surgeon by twelve years!

Although Dr. Dan did not make an official report of this operation until three and a half years later, the newspaper headlines sent the news around the world. "Sewed Up His Heart" read the headlines of the Chicago *Daily Inter-Ocean*. Williams was acclaimed as the first man in the world to "sew up the heart." Of course, his great contribution was the successful entrance of the chest and surgical exploration of the heart. His aseptic surgery was so perfect that no sign of infection appeared in the patient after the operation. His results were miraculous when one considers that he had very few of the advantages modern surgeons have today in their open-heart surgery and heart transplants.

Not long after his precedent-making heart operation, Williams learned that the position of chief surgeon at the Freedmen's Hospital in Washington, D.C., was open. This hospital with its two hundred beds as compared to the twelve beds at Provident Hospital offered new opportunities and broader challenges. Here he could help advance medical opportunities for Negroes on a national rather than a local scale. On September 17, 1893, he wrote to the Secretary of the Interior, Hoke Smith, applying for the position.

The Freedmen's Bureau was created in March, 1865, to help emancipated slaves adjust themselves to their new conditions. The Bureau turned to the pressing problems of Negro health and gave medical assistance to at least a million Negro patients. It established more than one hundred hospitals and dispensaries, among them the Freedmen's Hospital in Washington, D.C., erected on the grounds of Howard University. The first surgeon-in-chief was Dr. Robert Reyburn, who took over in 1868. In 1881 Dr. Charles B. Purvis was appointed surgeon-in-chief, the first Negro civilian in the United States to head a hospital under civilian auspices. He served for almost twelve years and was about to be replaced by the incoming Democratic administration.

Dr. Williams' application was endorsed by top medical men. It was also supported by Walter Gresham, the newly appointed Secretary of State. The author was surprised to come across a letter in the National Archives in Washington written by Frederick Douglass (supposedly a friend of Williams) urging the retention of Dr. Purvis in Freed-

Chicago, *February 10th 1894.*

This is to certify that Dr. Daniel H. Williams of Chicago has been well known to me about fourteen years, — as a medical student, as a practitioner and as a member of the Illinois State Board of Health. He is a very active and successful practitioner and of unexceptionable professional and social standing. He is competent to occupy any position that he will accept.

Wm. E. Quine
Prest Ill. State Board of Health;
Prest College Physicians & Surgeons.

Letter recommending Dr. Daniel H. Williams for the post of Surgeon-in-Chief of Freedmen's Hospital (February 10, 1894) men's Hospital as an "honest and able physician and a good and true man."[1] Nevertheless, Williams was appointed chief surgeon of Freedmen's Hospital in February, 1894.

To understand the situation at the time Williams took over at Freedmen's, it must be pointed out that the liberal period of Reconstruction was over and reaction had begun to set in. The Negro gradually began to lose his voting rights in the South and in parts of the North as well. Only the Freedmen's Hospital remained as a remnant of the liberal period and even that was threatened by indifference and neglect. Dr. Purvis, who had been in charge for the past twelve years, had been inefficient, medically behind the times, and had let things deteriorate badly. There were no trained nurses and the mortality rate was more than 10 percent.

Williams went to work. He reorganized the hospital into seven separate medical and surgical departments. He set up pathological and bacteriological departments in recognition of the new and more modern methods then being practiced. He set up a

[1] Douglass was the Haitian Commissioner at that time under a Republican administration. Dr. Purvis was also a Republican. Douglass's letter supporting Dr. Purvis could well have had political motivation as well as personal loyalty to the man. It was in favor of Dr. Purvis but not against Dr. Williams.

biracial staff of twenty of Washington's most competent specialists, who were willing to serve in the hospital without salary. He opened Freedmen's to outside white and black doctors. This was the first opportunity for many Negro doctors in Washington to gain hospital affiliation. He also set up the first internship program at Freedmen's Hospital, giving black interns an opportunity not afforded them at white hospitals.

Dr. Williams himself demonstrated and lectured in surgery, and while surgical cases increased almost 200 percent, the mortality rate dropped lower than 3 percent. By 1896 Freedmen's was admitting five hundred surgical cases per year and doctors from Johns Hopkins and the University of Pennsylvania were coming to watch Williams operate at clinics that he conducted.

As he had done at Provident Hospital, Williams set up a training program for nurses, which had high standards and requirements. Of five hundred applicants, fifty-nine were accepted, and by the end of the first month thirteen had been eliminated as unsatisfactory. The eighteen-month training course included instruction in diet, disinfection, antisepsis, and massage. Again, as at Provident, the program was a huge success.

Within the first year of Williams' arrival there

was a profound change in Freedmen's Hospital. New order and efficiency was apparent everywhere and the mortality rate went to an unprecedented low. The change was aptly described by Dr. William A. Warfield, one of the men whom Dr. Williams trained (later himself surgeon-in-chief of Freedmen's Hospital), who said, "Before Dr. Williams came to the hospital in 1894 there was no real surgical department. I was at the hospital three years before Dr. Williams and witnessed most of the surgical work, such as amputations of the thigh, leg, foot, and toes. It can be said that with the arrival of Dr. Williams surgical development began in all forms, especially abdominal. That is where I got my start and inspiration. Dr. Williams established a training school for nurses, replacing the old red-bandanna nurse. He appointed the first interns and brought into existence a horse ambulance. He was laying the foundation for more and better surgical work. By the time he left the hospital, a great impetus had been given to all branches of surgery."

Dr. Dan's political troubles began in 1896, when the Democrats lost the presidential election and the Republicans swept into power. Dr. Purvis, his Republican predecessor, instigated a Congressional investigation, hoping to oust Williams and replace him. Williams was completely exonerated.

However, political harassment followed, which was difficult for a man of Williams' temperament to endure, and on February 1, 1898, he tendered his resignation.

While in Washington Williams met and fell in love with Alice Johnson, the daughter of an ex-slave and the famous sculptor Moses Jacob Ezekiel. A few days after he resigned from Freedmen's Hospital, Dr. Dan, at the age of forty-two, married Alice Johnson. Paul L. Dunbar, Negro poet and friend of Dr. Dan, wrote a poem to commemorate the occasion. The poem reads in part:

> 'Tis no time for things unsightly,
> Life's the day and life goes lightly
> Science lays aside her sway
> Love rules Dr. Dan today
>
> Diagnosis, cease your squalling
> Check that scalpel's senseless bawling
> Put that ugly knife away
> Doctor Dan doth wed today

After their marriage Williams and his wife returned to Chicago, where he resumed his place as chief surgeon at Provident Hospital, now enlarged from twelve to sixty-five beds. As soon as they heard of his return, his former patients, black and white, flocked back. He became very active in his practice not only at Provident but at St. Luke's and Mercy hospitals as well. Because of his growing reputation as an outstanding surgeon he was frequently called to distant places—to North Dakota to perform surgery on a mining millionaire and to New York to attend a bishop of the Episcopal Church. On one occasion he was called to Tuskegee Institute by Booker T. Washington to perform an appendectomy on Washington's personal secretary.

In 1899 Dr. George W. Hubbard, president of Meharry Medical College, invited Williams to hold surgical clinics one week each year at Meharry. The annual Williams Clinics at Meharry were continued for many years and each was considered the great event of the school year. At Williams' urging, Nashville opened its own interracial hospital and thereby opened the whole field of modern surgery to Meharry students and doctors.

It was in Atlanta that Williams met Booker T. Washington, president of Tuskegee Institute and the most influential Negro leader at the time. Williams had come to Atlanta to meet with other Negro physicians from all over the country to organize the National Medical Association. Because of racial prejudice, it was virtually impossible for Negro physicians to join the American Medical Association. Williams was elected vice-president of the newly organized National Medical Association. Booker T. Washington had just made his famous Atlanta speech which alienated many Negro intellectuals because of its emphasis upon vocational rather than academic training for Negro youth. Williams urged Washington to build a medical and surgical center at Tuskegee that would serve the colored people of the South. He kept up a lively correspondence with Washington on this and other subjects concerning the medical care of the Negro. All of it came to naught. Washington was not interested.

Years after Williams had returned to Chicago, the Freedmen's Hospital was finally to be reorganized. Williams saw a great opportunity to build a really excellent hospital that would benefit Negroes all over the nation. He appealed to Booker T. Washington for help. At Washington's request, Williams submitted a list of several outstanding Negro physicians who, he felt, could run Freedmen's Hospital so as to make it a real contribution to Negro medicine. But in the meantime, Dr. Hall, his old enemy, had ingratiated himself with Booker Washington by means of political favors, and Washington asked Williams why he had left Dr. Hall's name off his list. Williams explained why he felt that Dr. Hall was not qualified. At that point Washington lost interest in Freedmen's Hospital and its reorganization and nothing was ever done.

Many Negro leaders felt that Booker T. Washington overemphasized industrial training and thereby neglected cultural education for the "Talented Tenth" (the 10 percent of Negro youth who were talented). They felt that Washington should push harder for the political rights of the Negro. While Williams felt that he had to work with Booker Washington, his heart and intelligence were with the protestors; those who, like his friend W. E. B. Du Bois, called and organized the Niagara Movement in 1905—the first formal organization to demand political and civil rights and the abolition of unequal economic opportunity for the Negro. Williams argued that "the ignorant and naturally suspicious will have to be gradually induced to relinquish their unquestioning faith in the infallible skill and judgment of the white man." He spoke like the militants in the Niagara Movement and its successor, the National Association for the Advancement of Colored People, when he said, "Those who toil get too little of the benefits of their labor, hence the power of the state should be used to regulate economic conditions and raise the living standards of the poor." Williams felt that political and social equality must arise from economic emancipation.

Dr. Hall had taken advantage of Dr. Williams' absence in Washington to advance himself at Provident Hospital by trickery and threats. Upon Williams' return, Hall made life unpleasant for him. The operating room would not be ready for him, nurses would not be detailed to him, his patients would be shown discourtesies. When in 1908 Negro physicians from all over the country gathered at a banquet in Chicago to celebrate Dr. Dan's twenty-fifth year in medicine, a silver bowl engraved with the names of thirty-seven Chicago doctors, black and white, was presented to Williams. Hall's name was not among them.

In 1912 Williams received the unprecedented honor of being appointed associate attending surgeon at St. Luke's Hospital in Chicago, an honor that no other member of his race would attain for twenty-five years after his death. St. Luke's was the largest, wealthiest, and most important hospital in Chicago at that time. Hall claimed that Williams' acceptance of this post was "an act of disloyalty to the Negro race" and succeeded in prevailing upon the Provident Hospital board to order Williams to bring all his patients to Provident. The order was absurd! Furthermore, it was insulting. Sorrowfully, Williams resigned from Provident.

Williams served at St. Luke's Hospital from his appointment in 1912 until his retirement from medicine. He ran one of the largest gynecological services in Chicago. His success at St. Luke's was so great that the hospital planned to name a ward after him. Wilberforce and Howard Universities conferred honorary degrees upon him. With the founding of the American College of Surgeons in 1913, Williams was among the charter members, the only Negro so honored. For many years he was a member of the exclusive Chicago Surgical Society and read papers before the organization and, by invitation, before numerous state and national scientific bodies.

In 1920 Williams built a summer home in beautiful Idlewild in the north Michigan woods. There he engaged in his favorite sports—swimming, fishing, and hunting. But it was not long before misfortune struck. One year after he built the summer home his wife, Alice, died of Parkinson's disease. Five years after his wife's death, Williams suffered a stroke which partially paralyzed him and effectively ended his medical career. Other strokes followed, complicated by the development of diabetes. Williams rallied and lived five years more, but his life was spent, and on August 4, 1931, he died at his summer home in Idlewild at the age of seventy-five.

In his will, Williams left his medical books to Mercy Hospital in Philadelphia, provision for his sisters, his brother's widow, his housekeeper, and his secretary, $2,000 for the colored YWCA in Washington, $2,000 for the operating room of a new interracial hospital on the South Side of Chicago, $5,000 each to Meharry and Howard Medical Schools to assist poor medical students, and $8,000 to the National Association for the Advancement of Colored People.

The world will remember Dr. Williams as a great American surgeon accorded top rank by his contemporary colleagues, white and black; as the founder of Provident Hospital, the first interracial hospital in the United States and forerunner of a hundred such institutions; as the first surgeon in the world to successfully enter the chest cavity; as the one who introduced the training of Negro nurses and interns in the United States; as a charter member of the American College of Surgeons; and finally, as one of the founders and first vice-president of the National Medical Association.

Louis Tompkins Wright
1891–1952

"The most productive, most important and most distinguished Negro physician yet to appear on the American scene," says the famous anthropologist, Dr. W. Montague Cobb. He was speaking of Dr. Louis T. Wright, a true pioneer in medicine—the first black physician to be appointed to the staff of a New York municipal hospital, the first black surgeon in the police department of New York City, the first to experiment with Aureomycin, an antibiotic, on humans, the first black surgeon to be admitted to the American College of Surgeons since its inception, and the first black physician in America to head a public interracial hospital. His daughter became the first black woman to be named dean of a medical school (New York Medical College).

Born in La Grange, Georgia, on July 23, 1891, Louis received his elementary, secondary, and

Louis Tompkins Wright, pioneer in clinical antibiotic research

college education at Clark University in Atlanta.
His father, Dr. Ceah Ketcham Wright, was a graduate of Meharry Medical College who, after a brief
medical practice, turned to the ministry. He died
when Louis was four years old, leaving his family
with little money. His mother had to find work, and

secured a job on the Clark University campus as matron in the girls' dormitory. This was about the time that Louis began school, and his early education was influenced by that brave band of New England men and women in Clark University who had gone South to teach in the religious schools. They were like the Peace Corps of today.

When Louis was eight years old, his mother married Dr. William Fletcher Penn, the first black man to graduate from Yale Medical School (1898). Dr. Penn was to have a profound influence on Louis's future. It was he who largely inspired and encouraged his desire to study medicine.

When Louis graduated from Clark University, he was the valedictorian of the class of 1911. When he went to Harvard Medical School to apply for admission, Dr. Otto Folin agreed to admit him if he could pass an examination in chemistry. Louis accepted the challenge. He went home and studied some chemistry books for two nights, came back and took the examination and passed with flying colors.

Evidence of Louis's unrelenting battle against racial discrimination was shown in his student years at Harvard. Told that he could not do his deliveries, as a student in obstetrics, at the Boston Lying-In Hospital, he replied that he had paid his tuition and was going to get what the catalogue called for: namely, deliveries at the Boston Lying-In Hospital. No "separate but equal" obstetrics for him! Needless to say, he got what he was entitled to, and the practice of having black students deliver babies with a black physician, separate from the rest of the class, was abolished.

At another time, when D. W. Griffith's film, *The Birth of a Nation*, described by many as racist and anti-Negro, was being shown at a theater in Boston, Louis left his studies at Harvard for three weeks to picket and protest the movie.

Summers were spent working as a field hand to make enough money to continue his studies at Harvard. In 1915 he graduated from Harvard Medical School, *cum laude*, and fourth in his class. His hatred of discrimination was shown by the following incident. After getting his M.D., he went to the courthouse in Georgia to register his medical license. "Sit on the bench," said the white clerk. When the call came, it was "Louis, Louis," but the doctor did not answer. The clerk came over and kicked his foot and said, "I was talking to you." "Not to me; my name is Dr. Louis T. Wright." Next came the call, "Wright, Wright," and again the doctor did not respond and again his foot was kicked. "I was talking to you." "Not to me, I am Dr. Louis

T. Wright." "Well," said the white man, "have you been peddling any dope or selling any abortions?" Wright stood up and looked him in the eye, saying, "Let me tell you something. I'll choke you right here if you open your Goddamned mouth again!"

In spite of graduating with honors, Wright was unable to get a Boston internship at such hospitals as Massachusetts General Hospital or Peter Bent Brigham Hospital because he was black. He did his internship at Freedmen's Hospital in Washington, D.C., a hospital for blacks. While there, he wrote a report of his work demonstrating that the Schick Test, for determining whether a person was susceptible to diphtheria, was valid in black people. It was the first original work done in and published from Freedmen's Hospital.

Here too, his fight against racism went on. He was sitting in the lobby of the hospital in his operating gown when a white man and woman came by. "Sam, where can I find the superintendent?" Wright replied, "Charlie, you find him yourself!" "Why, Goddamnit, I'm a U.S. senator." To which Wright replied, "Well, Goddamnit, it's high time you learned to call a doctor a doctor." The senator tried to have him dismissed. Like his predecessor, Dr. Daniel Hale Williams, Wright always insisted on the utmost respect toward the nurses. He almost lost his job when he demanded that a white man remove his hat in the obstetrical ward.

After his internship, Wright took medical examinations for licensing in three states. In Maryland, he received the highest mark of all who took the examination—94 percent. In Georgia, he again received the highest mark made by anyone that year—95.7 percent—and one of the highest marks ever made in that state. In New York, where the stiffest examination in the country is given, he got a mark of 92.4 percent. He returned to Atlanta, where he practiced for about one year before World War I broke out.

In 1917 Wright entered the U.S. Army as a first lieutenant in the Medical Corps. In the service, he introduced the intradermal method of vaccination for smallpox[1] that was adopted by the U.S. Army Medical Corps. In this method, he diluted the vaccine virus with saline (salt) solution and injected 0.1 cubic centimeters into, not through, the skin. This eliminated undesirable side reactions that were encountered in the "scratch" method. Later he was placed in charge of a base hospital in France, the

[1] L. T. Wright, "Intradermal Vaccination Against Smallpox," *Journal of the American Medical Association*, vol. 71, no. 8, August 18, 1918, pp. 654–657.

youngest surgeon to be given such responsibility. When the war ended, Wright was awarded the Purple Heart and discharged as a captain. Subsequently he rose to the rank of lieutenant colonel in the Medical Reserve Corps.

Wright's fight against discrimination and racism did not relax during his army service. It was said that at one time his colonel sent him to the front line for service in the expectation and hope that a "lucky" German bullet would take him away. Wright was a "burr under the saddle" to his white officer. But Wright escaped the bullets, although he was gassed, and he came back, whereupon the colonel was reported to have said, "Well, I sent you up there thinking you might be killed, but since you're back here you can take charge of the hospital because you're the best surgeon in the outfit." Needless to say, Wright did not thank him. He just walked out and took charge of the hospital. At another time, in France, Wright and a fellow officer had turned with drawn guns on white M.P.'s of another regiment who were going after them in the then popular pastime of shooting stray black soldiers.

The war over, Wright married Corinne Cooke on May 18, 1918, and opened an office for the practice of surgery in New York City. The following year, he was appointed at the lowest rung of the ladder at Harlem Hospital—clinical assistant visiting surgeon. At that time, Harlem was a wealthy white community and Wright was the first black physician to be appointed to the staff of the Harlem Hospital or any city hospital. Four white doctors resigned from the staff in protest. The following year, Wright was appointed to the surgical staff on a permanent basis. Twenty-three years later, he was to become director of surgery, and five years after that, president of the medical board.

In 1928 Wright took the competitive civil service examination for the position of police surgeon in New York City. Again his brilliance won him second place on the list, four-tenths of one percent behind the first man on the list! He was appointed to the position and thereby scored another first—the first black police surgeon in the history of New York City.

Wright specialized in surgery associated with head injuries and fractures. He devised a neck brace for fractures of the neck that is still in use today. He invented a special blade plate for the surgical treatment of fractures about the knee joint. He became such an authority in this area that he was asked to write the chapter on "Head Injuries" in the eleventh edition of Scudder's *Treatment of Frac-*

tures.[2] His chapter successfully challenged traditional theories on the treatment of such cases.

For his notable work in surgery, he was admitted in 1934 to fellowship in the American College of Surgeons, the first black physician to be admitted in twenty-one years. Dr. Daniel Hale Williams had been a charter member in 1913, and the only black member in all those years. In 1939, Wright became a diplomate of the American Board of Surgery. A diplomate is a physician who has been certified as a specialist by a board of professionals in his specialty.

In 1940 Wright was awarded the Spingarn Medal for his fight for racial equality and for his contributions to medical science.

As his widow told the writer, "Louis was not like today's specialists. He was a man who could think in many areas. His mind was so versatile about the whole human being that he could go into any area and find something creative to solve a problem in that area." And so it was that Wright's interests went beyond his surgical specialty. He was interested in, and became an authority on,

[2]Charles Scudder (editor), *Treatment of Fractures* (Philadelphia: W. B. Saunders Company, 11th edition, 1938), pp. 416–459.

lymphogranuloma venereum, a common veneral disease caused by a virus that can so weaken the body as to make the patient an invalid for life. When Dr. Subberow, an East Indian who knew Wright from his Harvard days, first isolated the antibiotic Aureomycin in the Lederle Laboratories, he brought a sample of it to Dr. Wright to try out on some of his lymphogranuloma patients. Thus Wright became the first physician in the world to experiment with this new antibiotic on humans, and the results were most successful.[3] He also experimented with another antibiotic, Terramycin. From 1948 to 1952, Wright published thirty papers dealing with Aureomycin research and eight with Terramycin research. Earlier publications dealt with traumatic conditions (accident injuries) and lymphogranuloma venereum. In all, he had eighty-nine scientific publications to his credit.

In 1948 his interests broadened further and he entered the field of cancer research. With the aid of grants from the National Cancer Institute and the Damon Runyon Fund, Wright founded the Harlem Hospital Cancer Research Foundation, where he

[3]L. T. Wright *et al*, "Aureomycin. A New Antibiotic with Virucidal Properties. A Preliminary Report on Successful Treatment in 25 Cases of Lymphogranuloma Venereum," *Journal of the American Medical Association*, vol. 38, no. 10, October 9, 1948, pp. 408–412.

dealt with the effectiveness of chemotherapeutic agents (chemicals that attack and destroy cancer cells) in the treatment of cancer. He published fifteen papers dealing with his investigations of the effects of such drugs as teropterin, triethylene melamine, folic acid, and hormones on cancer cells. One of these research efforts was performed together with his daughter, Dr. Jane Wright, who worked with him.[4] This daughter was later to take over the work herself. Chemotherapy today is widely used in the treatment of cancer.

In 1939 Wright was stricken with pulmonary tuberculosis, no doubt connected with his being gassed in France during the war. He was confined to bed for three years in Biggs Memorial Hospital in Ithaca, New York. A strong constitution and an indomitable will, together with expert medical care, brought him back to health and he returned to his work. He went on to become the director of surgery at Harlem Hospital in 1943 and the president of the medical board in 1948. In 1949 he was elected Fellow of the New York Surgical Society and in 1950 Fellow of the International College of Surgeons.

A militant fighter for equal rights for blacks,

[4]L. T. Wright and Jane Wright, "Further Observations on the Use of Triethylene Melamine in Neoplastic Diseases," *Archives of Internal Medicine*, March, 1952.

Wright led a constant and unflinching attack upon the injustices caused by racial barriers. In 1930 he had been the leader of a group of physicians who founded the Manhattan Medical Society. The society opposed the plan by the Rosenwald Fund to build separate hospitals for black people in New York. Wright maintained that "segregated hospitals represent a duality of citizenship in a democratic government that is wrong. Whenever colored hospitals are established, other hospitals in the community which have been admitting Negroes immediately begin to refuse admission to them, referring them to the colored hospital, which in many cases is rather small. Thus the Negro doctor would not be a physician to minister to the needs of all mankind irrespective of color, but he would be trained and taught that he is a Negro doctor—one who can treat only Negroes."

He also refused aid and grants from the Rosenwald Fund to build medical schools for the Negro. He felt that a school segregated along racial lines makes it inferior to others. Instead, he pleaded for the extension of good medical care to the entire population, equally and on a group basis. "This should be tax supported by the Federal Government," he declared, "and foundations handing out charity should be abolished as a menace to the practice of medicine." In 1932 he successfully opposed the erection of separate Veterans Hospitals for blacks in the North and any differential patterns whatever in medical care for veterans.

As for the American Medical Association, Wright felt that it had grown from a mild, academic body to a trade association of vast power. He opposed it, and held the association responsible for the inequalities in medical care. He condemned the association's silence on discrimination and the practice of it. Said Wright, "The American Medical Association has demonstrated as much interest in the health of the Negro as Hitler has in the health of the Jew." "Someday," he went on to say, "the nation will wake up to the fact that disease germs are not color conscious."

Wright attacked prejudice wherever he saw it, within the medical field or without. A prominent member of the National Association for the Advancement of Colored People and chairman of its board of directors, he was responsible for the establishment of the National Medical Committee within the NAACP to expose and oppose any form of racial segregation. He challenged the statement that Negroes had more syphilis, more tuberculosis, and more cancer than the whites. "The National Tuberculosis & Health Association," he wrote in *The*

Crisis,[5] "was unwilling to correct the real evils of poverty and prejudice. It only wished to limit disease among the Negroes so that they will not contaminate the whites." The NAACP under his chairmanship pressed a dozen investigations into discrimination in medical training and care.

In 1937 Dr. Wright was a sponsor of the Negro Peoples Committee that was formed to help the fight against fascism going on in Spain. The committee was affiliated with the North American Committee to Aid Spanish Democracy. Its letterhead bore this statement: "We representatives of a minority race recognize that our hope of freedom and equality is in combating Fascist theories and in achieving their liquidation both within and without our country."

On April 9, 1952, Dr. Wright received a citation from the John A. Andrews Memorial Hospital of Tuskegee Institute for his contributions to interracial health programs in the North and in the South. The citation read, "For his distinguished services in the cause of humanity, for resolute leadership of allied humanitarian and civic organizations dedicated to the advancement of social, economic, and related conditions basic to the health of all the people."

[5] L. T. Wright, "Factors Controlling Negro Health," *The Crisis*, vol. 42, no. 9, September, 1935.

Three weeks later, on April 30, 1952, he received a tribute in the form of a testimonial dinner given him at the Statler Hotel in New York City. The dinner was co-chaired by Dr. Ralph J. Bunche of the United Nations and Dr. Henry Cave, former president of the American College of Surgeons. Also present to pay tribute to Wright were Governor Dewey, Mayor Impellitteri, Hospitals Commissioner Kogel, and Walter White and Arthur Spingarn of the NAACP. Mrs. Franklin D. Roosevelt headed a list of speakers who lauded Dr. Wright for his achievements in medicine and civic work. He was presented with a portrait of himself.

Less than six months after that wonderful tribute, on October 8, 1952, Dr. Wright suffered a heart attack and died at the age of sixty-one. He was survived by his widow, Mrs. Corinne C. Wright, and two daughters, Dr. Jane Wright Jones and Dr. Barbara Wright Pierce, both physicians. Dr. Jane Wright Jones was the associate dean of New York Medical College, the first black woman in this high post. She is a cancer researcher and chemotherapist who succeeded her father as director of the Harlem Hospital Cancer Research Foundation. In 1964 she was appointed to the President's Commission on Heart Disease, Cancer and Stroke.

The new Harlem Hospital, a large, beautiful,

Dr. Wright's wife speaking at the dedication of Harlem Hospital's new
Louis T. Wright Surgical Building in New York City on October 30,
1969. Seated next to the painting of their father are Drs. Jane and
Barbara Wright.

modern, and well-equipped hospital, was named
after Dr. Wright and was dedicated on October 30,
1969—a fitting memorial to his more than thirty
years of outstanding work and service there. The
blood bank in this hospital was named after Dr.
Charles R. Drew, another pioneering black physician whose work on blood preservation made possible the blood banks in this country and elsewhere.

In an interview with the author, Mrs. Wright remembered her husband as a man who "had a mind that worked like a trigger all the time, on social as well as scientific problems. He did not think much of making money. I had no Cadillac, no mink coats. But we had all the books and food that we wanted.

"I think one of the remarkable things about Louis was that after many generations of trying to brainwash the Negro that he was an inferior person, there comes this group of young people who do not accept that. They have a great sense of their own dignity as human beings. Louis had it as a child of seven and eight.

"The first generation of educated Negroes had to be taught by whites. And that's why that whole group, Dr. Du Bois, Louis, and a whole group of them that came along, that would be anywhere from seventy-five to ninety now, that's how they got their education. Dr. Du Bois used to call them the Talented Tenth—ten percent of every group that is going to be better equipped mentally than other people. Dr. Du Bois felt that these people should be drained off and not sent to trade schools.

"Louis was motivated very early for high ideals. When he started at Harlem Hospital, he had no other ambition but to make Harlem Hospital the equal of Peter Bent Brigham at Harvard where the discipline and scientific work was of the highest. He had that vision and he had the vision that Negro doctors could do it, integrated in the hospital, as well as anybody else. This he spent his life proving and did prove before he died."

Charles Richard Drew
1904–1950

Of the millions of persons—soldiers and civilians—who received lifesaving blood transfusions, how many realize that they are alive today only because of the brilliant and pioneering work of an Afro-American physician? How many teachers and students of science know that it was Dr. Charles Richard Drew who organized the blood banks for both England and the United States during World War II? How is it that a discussion of blood banks in biology textbooks does not include Drew's critical work in that area?

It all began in a small, modest home in the ghetto area of Washington, D.C., when the midwife held up the newly born child and announced, "It's a boy!" The boy was Charles Drew and the day was June 3, 1904. He was the first of five children born to Richard Thomas Drew and Nora Burrell Drew. The father was a carpet layer and highly respected in

Charles Richard Drew, pioneer in blood plasma

the community. The mother was a graduate of the Miner Normal School, a teacher training institution.

The family lived in modest circumstances, and at the age of twelve Charles began to contribute to the family's finances by taking on a newspaper route. He was so successful and resourceful that it was not long before he had six other boys working for him. Young Drew attended public schools in Washington, graduating from Stevens Elementary School in 1918 and from Dunbar High School, with honors, in 1922.

Drew's extraordinary prowess in athletics manifested itself early, when he won a swimming tournament at the age of eight. At high school, he was a four-letter man, starring in football, basketball, baseball, and track. He won the James E. Walker Memorial Medal for all-around athletic performance.

At Amherst College, which he entered in 1922, he was a star on the freshman football team and the only member of the freshman class to win a major letter in track. In his junior year he was awarded the Thomas W. Ashley Memorial Trophy for being the team's most valuable football player. On graduation he received the Howard Hill Mossman Trophy as the man who contributed the most to Amherst in athletics during his four years in college. In 1924 he was mentioned as an All-American halfback in football.

It was at Amherst, however, that an incident involving racism and prejudice took place. The track team went to Brown University for a track meet. After the meet, the Amherst team was scheduled to eat together at a nearby hotel. To the amazement of Drew and three other Afro-Americans on the team the manager of the team informed them that the Narragansett Hotel would not serve the Afro-American members of the team. The four had to eat in the Brown University Commons while the rest of the team ate in luxury and comfort at the hotel. Needless to say, they left Brown embittered and resentful and Drew never forgot that incident.

Throughout his athletic career, Drew dreamed of going to medical school to become a physician, but money was always a problem. While attending Amherst, he had worked during the summers as a lifeguard at the segregated Francis Swimming Pools in Washington. After graduating from Amherst, he still did not have enough money for medical school and so he took a position at Morgan State College as director of athletics and teacher of biology. He stayed there for two years (1926–1928) and succeeded in bringing their football and basketball teams from very poor caliber to collegiate championship class.

For a while it looked as if Drew was embarked on a very promising career as an athletic director and college coach. However, he never forgot his early ambition and in 1928 he applied for admission to the Howard University School of Medicine. Because he had only six of the required eight hours of English at college, Howard refused him admission. They did offer him the post of assistant football coach with faculty status, but Drew refused.

He applied to McGill University Medical School in Canada and was accepted. There he turned out to be an outstanding student. It was as a student at McGill that Drew met and became friends with a young English doctor, John Beattie, who was his instructor in anatomy. Beattie did much to interest Drew in the problems of blood transfusion. Karl Landsteiner had just received the Nobel Prize (1930) for his work in blood grouping. He showed that all persons have one of four different types of blood: types A, B, AB, and O. To receive a blood transfusion successfully, the recipient and the donor must have the same type of blood and their bloods must be compatible; that is, nothing in the blood of one should cause the other's blood to coagulate or form a clot that would prevent the flow of blood in the body, thereby causing death. There are many factors in blood besides those that produce the four types. These other factors could cause the donor's and recipient's blood to be incompatible. This can easily be determined by a simple test called "cross matching" where a drop of the donor's blood is mixed on a glass slide with a drop of the recipient's blood. If no coagulation or "clumping" takes place, the two bloods are compatible.

Both Drew and Beattie were concerned about the loss of life due to lack of available blood when needed. Drew saw many cases where patients died because of a loss of large amounts of blood following an accident or a surgical operation. These patients could have been saved if blood were given to them promptly. At that time, however, by the time the patient's blood was typed, a donor of the right type sought and found, his blood drawn, and the blood given to the patient, it was often too late. There was a critical need for blood to be preserved, stored, and ready for instant use. This was the problem that Drew and Beattie were to be concerned with during World War II—Beattie in London and Drew in New York.

Things looked pretty bad for Drew in his third year at McGill. His money ran out when he had one more year to go. It began to look as if he would not be able to complete his medical education. The year was 1931, a Depression year, and jobs were hard to find. When things were at their worst, a wonderful thing happened. He received a Rosenwald Fellowship from the Julius Rosenwald Foundation which enabled him to complete his medical education and finish second in a class of 137 students. He won the annual prize in neuroanatomy and the Williams Prize in his senior year on the basis of a competitive examination given to the top five students in the graduating class. He was also elected to Alpha Omega Alpha, the medical honorary scholastic fraternity.

On graduation from McGill, Drew interned for one year at the Montreal General Hospital in Canada. During this period he frequently worked with Beattie, who was continuing his research on blood transfusion, and Drew's interest in that area grew. He completed his internship in 1935, and went to Howard University Medical School as an instructor in pathology. Beattie returned to England, where war clouds were gathering. Hitler had rejected the Treaty of Versailles and seemed bent on conquering Europe and the world.

Drew's goal at Howard was to set up a program of surgical resident training at the Freedmen's

Hospital, the teaching hospital of Howard Medical School, that would at least equal if not surpass the training available to white residents in other hospitals. His work there was so outstanding that he soon became assistant in surgery and then assistant surgeon at the hospital.

The turning point in Drew's life came when, at the recommendation of the Dean, he was granted a research fellowship by the Rockefeller Foundation's General Education Board. Drew jumped at the chance. Here was his opportunity to pursue the interest he had acquired at McGill, to do research in blood and blood transfusion. He spent two years (1938–1940) in graduate study at Columbia University in New York and as resident in surgery in the Presbyterian Hospital connected with Columbia's School of Medicine. There he worked with Dr. Scudder. Scudder's team was engaged in studies relating to fluid balance, blood chemistry, and blood transfusion, particularly as they related to "surgical shock." In cases of shock, the blood pressure drops and the pulse grows weak due to an upset in the control of blood flow through the body. The patient may lose consciousness and, if the condition is not promptly corrected, he may even die. Shock is common with severe wounds. It may also follow surgery where a large amount of blood may be lost.

As a surgeon, Drew was very much interested in shock. In a research report,[1] Drew pointed out that in surgical shock the capillaries of the body dilate (get larger), leading to a decrease in the circulation of blood in the body. This, in turn, leads to a lowering of the blood pressure. One of the measures he recommended for treating surgical shock was to give the patient adequate amounts of blood or blood plasma.

It is known that blood that is withdrawn from the body quickly spoils and is difficult to preserve. At Columbia, Drew's special field of study was the preservation of blood so as to have it immediately available when needed. He set up experiments to study all the factors—physical, chemical, and biological—that produced changes in blood when drawn from the body. Such changes often made the blood unfit for transfusion. Drew's hours were long and this pioneering work was difficult, but the results were indeed rewarding. At one point he tried plasma alone, with very good results. Plasma is the liquid portion of the blood without the cells. Plasma could be stored for a long time without spoiling, whereas whole blood, at Drew's time, could be stored

[1] C. R. Drew, "The Early Recognition and Treatmen of Shock," *Anesthesiology*, March, 1942.

for only one week. Furthermore, when using plasma, blood typing was not necessary and cross matching was not required. Anybody could be given the plasma from any other person. This, of course, was most important on the battlefield where time was critical in saving the life of a badly wounded soldier.

The idea of blood banks was not new. Research in this area had been carried on in the United States and in other parts of the world. In a report, Drew referred to the work done by Soviet scientists:

> To them must go the credit for supplying the early work, most of the fundamental knowledge, and the impetus which has to a large degree been responsible for the widespread creation of the blood and plasma banks which have played and are playing such a tremendous role in reducing the number of deaths on the battlefields of the world.[2]

In this report he also referred to the work done in 1936 by Dr. Duran Jorda, who organized what was then considered the best system of collection and distribution of blood for the Republican Army of

[2] C. R. Drew, "The Role of Soviet Investigators in the Development of the Blood Bank," *American Review of Soviet Medicine*, April, 1944.

Spain. Dr. Jorda used glucose citrate to prevent clotting in donated blood.

The term "blood bank" was coined by Dr. Bernard Fantus in March 1937. He instituted, at the Cook County Hospital in Chicago, a system built around the principle of having a central depot in the hospital where donors could be sent to have blood drawn and stored for future use.

Drew threw himself into his work with enthusiasm and determination. He collected all available information in the area of blood and plasma preservation. He experimented with all the important aspects of blood collection, preservation, transfusion, and blood chemistry. As his published reports and doctoral thesis indicate, he became an authority on the subject.

In the midst of his work, Drew was invited by the Dean of Howard Medical School to present a report on blood transfusion at the annual meeting of the John T. Andrews Memorial Clinic to be held at the Tuskegee Institute in Alabama on April 6, 1939. Drew felt highly honored and accepted the invitation. He drove down with a group of fellow doctors, who decided to stop over for one night in Atlanta. At a home there, near Spelman College, he met and fell in love with a home economics teacher, Lenore Robbins. Four days later, on his way back from Tuskegee, he stopped off again, this time to propose marriage. He was accepted and the marriage took place on September 23, 1939.

Back at Columbia, Drew and Scudder worked toward setting up a blood bank at the Presbyterian Hospital that would provide blood in emergencies, and at the same time they investigated the safest and best methods of preserving blood for transfusion. This would give them the opportunity to study the physical, chemical, and biological changes that take place in blood when it is stored. They planned to experiment with different types of containers as well, and with different methods of preventing the clotting of blood outside the body. The blood bank was established in August 1939.

Drew became more convinced that plasma was better than whole blood for transfusions. With plasma, he found none of the reactions that were still occurring with the use of whole blood. Chemical breakdown and hemolysis (dissolving) of the red blood cells were the stumbling blocks in trying to store blood for long periods of time. Drew found that shortly after blood was taken from a donor, potassium ions (the element potassium in combination with other chemical elements is known as a potassium ion) are released from the red blood cells into the plasma. This was proving to be toxic or poisonous to the body of the recipient. The longer the blood was stored, the more potassium ions were released into the plasma. Drew's experiments not only demonstrated these facts but also showed that refrigeration and careful handling of the donated blood could slow down this process to some extent.

Money for continuing these experiments was running out when, in January 1940, because of Drew's remarkable work, the Blood Transfusion Association made funds available to the Presbyterian Hospital for carrying on laboratory and clinical studies on the preservation of plasma and its use as a blood substitute. Drew was able to carry on his work.

In the meantime World War II had started. France was being seriously threatened. The Maginot Line was not as impregnable as it was thought to be. Casualties began to mount and France did not have enough blood for her wounded. In the spring of 1940 an emergency meeting was called by the Blood Transfusion Association. The top blood experts of the country were invited, including two Nobel Prize winners—Dr. Alexis Carrel, who won the prize for his blood vessel surgery and transplant of organs, and Dr. Karl Landsteiner of "blood group" fame. Drew was invited as an authority on blood and blood plasma. With the backing of Landsteiner, Drew convinced the group that shipping and using plasma instead of whole blood for transfusion was more practical and effective. The "Plasma for France" program was set up. But it was too late. On June 14, 1940, German troops had marched into Paris and hardly more than a week later an armistice was signed by the Vichy government.

During his stay at Columbia, Drew decided to register for the Doctor of Science degree (Sc.D.) in medicine. No black physician had ever been granted this degree, but that did not deter Drew. In fact, it made him all the more determined to explode the myth of white superiority. His doctoral thesis, "Banked Blood: A Study in Blood Preservation," was described by Dr. Scudder as a "monumental work and a guide to the founding of blood banks." It dealt with the evolution of the blood bank, the known changes that take place in preserved blood, his experimental studies in blood preservation, and the organization, operation, and success of the blood bank at the Presbyterian Hospital. Drew received the Sc.D. degree from Columbia in 1940—the first Negro to receive this degree in the country.

At the same time, Drew took the examination to become certified as a diplomate of the American Board of Surgery, a physician who is certified as a specialist by a board of specialists in his field. Again Drew was successful and in 1941 became one of

The Howard University Medical Unit headed by Dr. Charles Drew is shown instructing nurses in the treatment of air-raid victims during a practice raid in Washington, D.C.

After first aid has been administered, the air raid "victim" is removed to the hospital by the Office of Civilian Defense's medical unit.

the very few Negroes in the country to become a diplomate in surgery.

His work in New York completed, Drew returned to Howard Medical School. However, it was not to be for long. By 1940 the war in England had been going on for nearly a year and the military situation was growing worse. The German blitz over London was taking its toll among military and civilians alike. The number of wounded was growing daily and there simply was not enough blood for transfusions. The Blood Transfusion Association that was instrumental in setting up the short-lived "Plasma for France" program now offered its help to Great Britain, and in August, 1940, the "Blood for Britain" project was organized.

Trouble developed very shortly. Each of the hospitals involved in the project used their own methods for collecting and processing the blood. No uniform standards were set. As a result, much of the plasma reaching England was contaminated and useless. It became obvious that organization was imperative and somebody had to be in charge.

It was at this time that Drew received a cablegram from his former teacher at McGill, Dr. John Beattie. Beattie was then director of research laboratories of the Royal College of Surgeons in England and in charge of shock treatment and transfusions for the Royal Air Force. His cablegram read:

COULD YOU SECURE 5,000 AMPULES DRIED PLASMA FOR TRANSFUSION WORK IMMEDIATELY AND FOLLOW THIS BY EQUAL QUANTITY IN THREE TO FOUR WEEKS STOP CONTENTS EACH AMPULE SHOULD REPRESENT ABOUT ONE PINT WHOLE PLASMA.

This cablegram was followed shortly by a telegram from the Blood Transfusion Association in New York:

THE BOARD HAS DECIDED TO CREATE A POSITION OF FULL-TIME MEDICAL SUPERVISOR TO ACT AS LIAISON OFFICER BETWEEN THE BOARD AND THE HOSPITALS ENGAGED IN PROCESSING PLASMA FOR SHIPMENT TO THE BRITISH RED CROSS. I AM REQUESTED TO OFFER THIS POSITION AND ALL IT INVOLVES TO YOU AS BEING THE BEST QUALI-FIED OF ANYONE WE KNOW TO ACT IN THIS IM-PORTANT DEVELOPMENT.

Drew accepted and left immediately for New York. There were many technical problems connected with this pioneering experiment and they had to be solved before the mass production of plasma was attempted. The first thing he did was to standardize procedures at all the participating hospitals for collecting and processing blood so as to avoid contamination. This alone resulted in a dramatic reduction in spoiled blood plasma arriving in England. The handling of volunteer donors was another problem. Some hospitals had more volunteers than they could handle while others did not have enough donors. Drew set up a central depot in the New York Academy of Medicine building on Fifth Avenue where volunteers could call in and be assigned to one of the participating hospitals. Appeals for donors were made on the radio and through the newspapers (there was no television at that time). Thousands volunteered their blood. The project was a huge success.

The American Red Cross joined the "Blood for Britain" project. By the end of 1940 the British were operating their own blood donor centers and no longer needed our help. The last shipment of blood went to England on January 17, 1941. With the ending of the British project, the American Red Cross decided to set up a nationwide program to collect blood for the American armed forces. Drew was appointed director of the new project. Blood donor stations were set up all over the country and again the response was excellent.

Suddenly a bombshell struck. The armed forces

informed the American Red Cross that "colored" blood would not be acceptable. Protests came from all parts of the country, resulting in a modification of this policy: Negro blood would be accepted but would be segregated! In a newspaper article, Albert Deutsch wrote:

At the very time Drew was setting up this Red Cross blood bank, helping to save thousands of American lives through his brilliant scientific and administrative work, his blood would have been rejected by the Red Cross had he offered to donate it. Later, when the Red Cross modified its policy and accepted Negro blood on a Jim Crow basis, his blood would have been segregated with that of other Negroes.[3]

Under the headline, "Negro Surgeon, World Plasma Expert, Derides Red Cross Blood Segregation," a Chicago newspaper had the following to say:

No Negro blood accepted but—
When the terrible blitz raids of London in September 1940 killed and wounded thousands and an emergency call went out to

[3]*PM*, March 30, 1944

2 3 7

America for dried blood for transfusions, it was an American Negro surgeon to whom English medical men appealed to organize and send U.S. blood plasma overseas.

No Negro blood accepted but—

When the American Red Cross set up its first blood collection center in New York for our own armed forces, it was a Negro surgeon who was selected to supervise the entire project and expand the system to every city in the U.S.

No Negro blood accepted but—

When the Japanese bombed Pearl Harbor and maimed hundreds of American soldiers and sailors, it was blood collected by a Negro surgeon that saved their lives.[4]

In the same newspaper, Drew attacked the ruling of the armed forces as indefensible from any point of view—scientific or otherwise. He said:

The question arises—is there a difference between the blood of different races? Is it possible to transmit the traits and characteristics of one

[4]Chicago *Defender*, September 26, 1942.

race to a member of another race by means of blood transfusion?

One cannot say that there are no differences in bloods of different races. But one can say without any hesitation that no difficulties have been shown to exist between the bloods of different races which would in any way counter-indicate the use of the blood from one individual of one race to an individual of another race for the purpose of transfusion providing the bloods were of the same group.

There are many who have a real fear born of ignorance that the blood of a Negro carries with it the possibility of their offspring having dark skin and other characteristics of the Negro race. Only extensive education, continued wise government and an increasing fight on our part to disseminate the scientific facts and raise our levels of achievement can overcome this prejudice which to a large extent is founded on ignorance.

Some say that Drew left blood work because of this policy of segregating Negro blood. His widow told the author, however, "He did not want to get sidetracked and wanted to get back to surgery—his primary interest." At any rate, Drew returned to

Howard Medical School in May, 1941, and to his resident training program in surgery at the Freedmen's Hospital.

Because of his extraordinary ability, it was not long before he was elevated to a full professorship and head of the department of surgery at Howard, and chief of surgery at the Freedmen's Hospital. In 1944 he was appointed chief of staff of the hospital. Shortly thereafter he was given the unique distinction of being made an examiner by the American Board of Surgery, a position never before held by a Negro.

Awards and honors followed. In 1944 Drew received the much coveted Spingarn Medal, given by the National Association for the Advancement of Colored People, for his work on blood plasma. This was followed by the E. S. Jones Award for Research in Medical Science. In 1946 he was elected Fellow of the International College of Surgeons. In 1949 he was appointed Surgical Consultant for the U.S. Army's European Theater of Operation. He was a member of a team of four physicians who toured hospital installations in occupied Europe to improve the quality of these hospitals. In 1945 Drew received the honorary degree of Doctor of Science from Virginia State College as well as from his alma mater, Amherst College.

The tragic and unforeseen end came on April 1, 1950, when he was in his prime. Drew was scheduled to attend a medical clinic at the Tuskegee Institute in Alabama. Three of his residents from Freedmen's Hospital were going with him. Drew had planned to go by train, but his residents could not afford the train fare. Since Drew was anxious to have them go, he decided to drive them to Alabama by auto. He had been a speaker at a meeting the previous evening and so it wasn't until two o'clock in the morning that the four left Washington for Alabama. Drew was driving and he was so tired from lack of sleep that he dozed off for a moment. The auto went off the road. When he tried to straighten it out, the auto overturned. Drew was killed, but the three doctors traveling with him were not hurt.

Drew's death left his family financially unprepared. There was little money in the bank and government insurance provided only a small pension for his wife and four children. Friends came to the aid of the family by creating the Charles R. Drew Memorial Fund. Financial aid also came from Howard Medical School and the University administration. Drew's alma mater, Amherst College, set up a tuition fund for his daughter, Charlene, at Oberlin College.

Comments by those who knew Drew well tell a

good deal about the kind of man he was. To quote a colleague, "Charlie never made over five thousand dollars a year in his life but he was always taking money out of his own pocket to help needy medical students or residents." Dr. Burke Syphax said of Drew, "He had offers of up to twenty thousand dollars a year from drug companies to head research projects. Although Dr. Drew believed in eventual integration, he wanted to demonstrate that Negro-trained students could make equally fine doctors." Albert Deutsch paid Drew the following tribute, "Handsome, modest, well-endowed both physically and mentally, he is a living refutation of the myth of white supremacy. He has fought his way up through the dense mass of discrimination that only a Negro knows. He is all-American caliber, a man deserving homage from all, black and white."

A touching tribute came from Drew's former coach at Amherst College, D. O. "Tuss" McLaughry, in an article in the *Saturday Evening Post* of December 1952.[5]

[5]"The Best Player I Ever Coached"

In all of Amherst College's long history, no campus generation treasures a more glorious football memory than the graduates of 1923–26. Easily their most memorable thrill while I coached there was given them by a tall, well-built Negro halfback from Washington, D.C., named Charlie Drew. And he did it as a sophomore.

Dr. W. Montague Cobb of Howard Medical School, a leading anthropologist and a classmate of Drew's at Amherst as well as his teammate on the track team there, said of Drew, "In his teaching and ward work, Dr. Drew was dynamic and inspirational. His greatest emphasis was upon physiological surgical principles. It may be safely said that as a result of his unrelenting efforts, modern surgery with a progressive outlook is firmly established in the Howard Medical Center."

Near the close of the 1923 season, Amherst was trailing hopelessly behind Wesleyan. On the last play of the game, Drew tried a desperate pass. With tacklers hanging all over him, he got off a tremendous forty-yard throw to McBride. It was good for a touchdown and a precious 12-10 victory. Better still, it built up such team faith in Drew that he was able to lead Amherst to its largest scores in Little Three history at its peak in 1925, two seasons later. That year Amherst lost only to Princeton and even in losing Drew gained more than 160 yards and was the outstanding man on the field. The winning streak continued strong through 1926, after Drew and I had left.

One hint of Drew's phenomenal speed, for the benefit of those who never saw him in action, is the fact that when this six-foot-one, 195-pounder turned to track, he won the junior national A.A.U. hurdles championship.

In football, he was lighting-fast on the getaway and dynamite on inside plays, plowing on with a "second effort" that brought him yardage long after he should have been stopped. He threw the old pumpkin-shaped ball farther and with more accuracy than anyone else I ever saw, and was also an excellent receiver. He was equally effective on defense, a true tackler and pass stopper.

As Dr. Charles R. Drew, he went on to an eminent medical career until cut down tragically in the spring of 1950. But to Amherst men, he will go on and on in memory, as he did on the field.

In describing her husband to the author, Mrs. Drew remembers him as a hearty man who loved to romp with his children, sing, and play the piano, saxophone, and even the ukelele. She stressed his powerful personality and said that he had a profound influence on others. He spent a lot of time and effort on training his residents in surgery and set up an excellent program for them. "Charlie was just too good for his own good," Mrs. Drew said. "Giving people the shirt off his back was his favorite pastime."

Drew's name will not be forgotten. Schools in Washington, D.C., Wilmington, Delaware, Arlington, Virginia, and in Florida, Texas, Illinois, and Indiana have been named after him. A medical center in California bears his name. There is the Drew dormitory at Howard University. In September 1968, the Charles R. Drew Neighborhood Health Center was opened in the Bedford-Stuyvesant section of Brooklyn, New York.

Every blood bank in the country and in the world is a living memorial and a tribute to the genius of Dr. Charles Richard Drew.

Bibliography

BENJAMIN BANNEKER

Allen, W. W., and Murray, D. *Banneker the Afro-American Astronomer.* Privately published by the authors. Washington, D.C.: 1921.

Aptheker, H. *A Documentary History of the Negro People in the United States.* New York: Citadel Press, 1951.

Brawley, Benjamin. *Negro Builders and Heroes.* Chapel Hill: University of North Carolina, 1937.

Butterfield, Roger. "An Intellectual Argued with a Founding Father." *Life* Magazine (November 22, 1968).

Dobler, L., and Toppin, E. A. *Pioneers and Patriots: The Lives of Six Negroes of the Revolutionary Era.* Garden City, N.Y.: Doubleday, 1965.

Downing, Lewis K. "Contributions of Negro Scientists." *The Crisis,* vol. 46, no. 6 (June 1939).

Franklin, John H. *From Slavery to Freedom.* 2nd edition, revised. New York: Knopf, 1956.

Historical Society of Pennsylvania. *Records 1790–1901.* The Banneker Institute is among the organizations represented in this collection.

Graham, Shirley. *Your Most Humble Servant.* New York: Julian Messner, 1949.

Latrobe, John H. "Memoir of Benjamin Banneker." *Maryland Colonization Journal* (May 1845).

Padover, Saul K. "Benjamin Banneker, Unschooled Wizard." *The New Republic* (February 2, 1948).

Tyson, Martha E. *Banneker, the Afro-American Astronomer*. Philadelphia: Friends Book Association, 1884.

Woodson, Carter, and Wesley, C. H. *Story of the Negro Retold*. 4th ed., Washington, D.C.: Associated Publishers, 1959.

GEORGE WASHINGTON CARVER

Bontemps, Arna W. *The Story of George Washington Carver*. New York: Grosset & Dunlap, 1954.

Borth, Christy. *Pioneers of Plenty—The Story of Chemurgy*. New York: Bobbs-Merrill, 1942.

Campbell, Thomas M. *The Movable School Goes to the Negro Farmer*. Alabama: Tuskegee Institute Press, 1926.

Carver, G. W. "The Undiscovered Sweet Potato." *Agricultural Digest*, vol. 2, no. 11 (April 1918).

Carver, G. W. "Many Food Products Can Be Made from Peanuts and Sweet Potato." *American Food Journal* (August 1921).

Carver, G. W. Statement at Hearings before Committee on Ways and Means, House of Representatives, on Schedule G, Agricultural Products and Provisions, Tariff Information, 1921. Washington, D.C.: Government Printing Office, 1921.

Childers, James S. "A Boy Who Was Traded for a Horse." *American Magazine* (October 1932).

Clark, Glenn. *The Man Who Talks with Flowers*. St. Paul, Minn.: Macalester Park Publishing Company, 1938.

Curtis, Austin W. "Forty Years of Creative Research Work." *Peanut Journal and Nut World*, Suffolk, Va. (March 1937).

Epstein, Sam. *George Washington Carver: Negro Scientist*. Champaign, Ill.: Garrard, 1960.

Graham, Shirley, and Lipscomb, G. D. *Dr. George Washington Carver, Scientist*. New York: Julian Messner, 1944.

Holt, Rackham. *George Washington Carver*. Garden City, N.Y.: Doubleday, 1943.

Moss, Wade W. "The Wizard of Tuskegee." *The Chemist* (October 1936).

National Archives. Washington, D.C. General Records, Agriculture Department, 1839–1943, R.G. 16, Carver correspondence.

National Archives. Washington, D.C. Office of Experimental Stations 1888–1937, R.G. 164, Work of Carver at the Tuskegee Experimental Station, Tuskegee Institute.

Ovington, Mary W. *Portraits in Color*. New York: Viking Press, 1927.

Wright, C. W. "Negro Pioneers in Chemistry." *School and Society*, vol. 65 (February 1, 1947).

CHARLES RICHARD DREW

Cobb, W. Montague. "Charles Richard Drew, M.D." *Journal of the National Medical Association*, vol. 42, no. 4 (July 1950).

Drew, C. R. *et al*. Report Concerning the Project for Supplying Blood Plasma to England. New York: Blood Transfusion Association (June 1941).

Drew, C. R. "Negro Scholars in Scientific Research." *Journal of Negro History* (April 1950).

Drew, C. R. "The Early Recognition and Treatment of Shock." *Anesthesiology* (March 1942).

Drew, C. R. "The Role of Soviet Investigators in the Development of the Blood Bank." *American Review of Soviet Medicine* (April 1944).

Downing, Lewis K. "Contributions of Negro Scientists." *The Crisis*, vol. 46, no. 6 (June 1939).

Embree, E. R., and Waxman, J. *Investment in People: The Story of the Julius Rosenwald Fund*. New York: Harper, 1949.

Hepburn, David. "The Life of Dr. Charles R. Drew." *Our World*, vol. 5, no. 23 (July 1950).

McLaughry, D. O. "The Best Player I Ever Coached." *Saturday Evening Post* (December 6, 1952).

Richardson, Ben. *Great American Negroes*. New York: T. Y. Crowell, 1956.

Sterne, Emma G. *Blood Brothers: Four Men of Science*. New York: Knopf, 1959.

Stratton, M. R. *Negroes Who Helped Build America*. Boston: Ginn, 1965.

Truax, Rhoda. *True Adventures of Doctors*. Boston: Little, Brown, 1954.

Who's Who in Colored America, 1950.

LLOYD A. HALL

Adams, R. L. *Great Negroes Past and Present*. Chicago: Afro-American Publishing Company, 1964.

American Men of Science. 7th edition, 1944.

Bardolph, Richard. *The Negro Vanguard*. New York: Rinehart, 1959.

Downing, Lewis K. "Contributions of Negro Scientists." *The Crisis*, vol. 46, no. 6 (June 1939).

Guzman, J. P., ed. *The Negro Yearbook*. New York: William H. Wise, 1952.

Hall, L. A. "The Negro in Chemistry." *School and Society*, vol. 52 (July 6, 1940).

Hall, L. A. "The Time Has Come." *Food Technology*, vol. 11, no. 10 (1957).

"A Man We Can't Forget." *Chemical and Engineering News*, vol. 37 (January 26, 1959).

PERCY L. JULIAN

Davis, Elizabeth L. *Fathers of America*. Old Tappan, N.J.: Revell, 1958.

DeKruif, Paul. "The Man Who Wouldn't Give Up." *Readers Digest* (August 1946).

Embree, E. R., and Waxman, J. *Investment in People: The Story of the Julius Rosenwald Fund*. New York: Harper, 1949.

Fosdick, Franklin. "New Hope for Old Men." *Negro Digest* (March 1951).

Geiser, S. W. "America's Leading Soy Bean Chemist." *Opportunity*, vol. 19, no. 3 (March 1941).

Gilman, H. *Organic Chemistry*. vol. 2. New York: John Wiley, 1943.

Janson, Donald. "Wealthy Negroes Buoy Rights Drive." *The New York Times* (April 30, 1968).

Julian P. L., and Pikl, Josef. "Indole Series (III) Synthesis of Physostigmine." *Journal of the American Chemical Society*, vol. 57, no. 3 (March 1935).

Taylor, J. H., ed. *The Negro in Science*. Baltimore: Morgan State College Press, 1955. (Section by H. R. Branson.)

Ward, Lawrence. "America's Leading Soy Bean Expert." *Journal of Negro Life*, vol. 19, no. 3 (March 1941).

Wormley, S. L., and Fenderson, L. H., eds. *Many Shades of Black*. New York: William Morrow, 1969. (Chapter by Julian.)

Wright, Clarence W. "The Negro in Science." *Industrial Trends*, vol. 6, no. 2 (October 1949).

ERNEST E. JUST

Downing, Lewis K. "Contributions of Negro Scientists." *The Crisis*, vol. 46, no. 6 (June 1939).

Dover, Cedric. "Not Genetics but Pettersson." *Modern Education.* (July–August 1950).

Just, E. E. *The Biology of the Cell Surface.* Philadelphia: P. Blakiston, 1939.

Just, E. E. *Basic Methods for Experiments in Eggs of Marine Animals.* Philadelphia: P. Blakiston, 1939.

Karpman, Ben. Obituary on Just. *Journal of Nervous and Mental Diseases* (February 1943).

Lillie, Frank R. Obituary on Just. *Science* (January 2, 1942).

McKean, Else. *Up Hill.* New York: Shady Hill Press, 1947.

Nabrit, Milton S. "Profile: Just." *Phylon*, vol. 7, no. 2 (1946).

Ovington, Mary W. *Portraits in Color.* New York: Viking Press, 1927.

LEWIS H. LATIMER

Edison Pioneers. *Tribute to Latimer.* New York: 1928.

Latimer, L. H. *Incandescent Electric Lighting.* New York: D. Van Nostrand, 1890.

Negro History Associates. *The Story of Lewis Latimer.* New York: 1964.

Ploski, H. A., and Brown, R. C. *Negro Almanac.* New York: Bellwether Publishing Company, 1967.

JAN MATZELIGER

Baker, Henry. *The Colored Inventor.* Crisis Publishing Company, 1913.

Kaplan, Sidney. "Jan Ernst Matzeliger and the Making of the Shoe." *Journal of Negro History*, vol. 40, no. 1 (January 1955).

Rollins, C. H. *They Showed The Way*. New York: T. Y. Crowell, 1964.

ELIJAH MCCOY

Baker, Henry. *The Colored Inventor*. Crisis Publishing Company, 1913.

Turner, Arthur, and Moses, Earl R. *Colored Detroit: A Brief History of Detroit's Colored Population*. Detroit: 1924.

GARRETT A. MORGAN

Adams, Russell. *Great Negroes Past and Present*. Chicago: Afro-American Publishing Company, 1963.

Davis, Russel H. *Memorable Negroes in Cleveland's Past*. Cleveland: Western Reserve Historical Society, 1969.

"Garrett A. Morgan." *The Crisis*, vol. 7, no. 4 (February 1914).

Who's Who of the Colored Race, vol. 1 (1915).

NORBERT RILLIEUX

Meade, G. P. "A Negro Scientist of Slavery Days." *Negro History Bulletin*, vol. 20, no. 7 (April 1957).

Rollins, C. H. *They Showed the Way*. New York: T. Y. Crowell, 1964.

Wright, Clarence W. "The Negro in Science." *Industrial Trends*, vol. 6, no. 2 (October 1949).

"The American Negro as an Inventor." *Negro History Bulletin*, vol. 3, no. 6 (March 1940).

DANIEL HALE WILLIAMS

Buckler, Helen. *Doctor Dan: Pioneer in American Surgery*. Boston: Little, Brown, 1954.

Cobb, W. Montague. "Dr. Daniel H. Williams—Pioneer and Innovator." *Journal of the National Medical Association*, vol. 45, no. 5 (September 1953).

Dailey, U. G. Obituary—Daniel Hale Williams, M.D. *Journal of the National Medical Association*, vol. 23, no. 4 (October 1931).

French, R. *Biographies of Eminent American Physicians and Surgeons.* Indianapolis: Stone, 1894.

Kenny, J. A. "Dr. Daniel Williams Takes Priority in Successful Operation for Stab Wound of Human Heart." *Journal of the National Medical Association*, vol. 27 (1935).

Link, Eugene, P. "The Civil Rights Activities of Three Great Negro Physicians, 1840–1940." *Journal of Negro History*, vol. 52, no. 3 (July 1967).

Morais, Herbert M. *The History of the Negro in Medicine.* New York: International Library of Negro Life and History, 1967.

National Archives. Washington, D.C. General Records, Interior Department, 1849–1943 R. G. 48, Records of Appointment Division, letters pertaining to Williams.

Redding, Saunders. *The Lonesome Road.* Garden City, N.Y.: Doubleday, 1958.

Richardson, Clement. *The National Cyclopedia of the Colored Race*, vol. 1. Montgomery, Ala.: 1919.

Stratton, M. R. *Negroes Who Helped Build America.* Boston: Ginn, 1965.

Watson, I. A. *Physicians and Surgeons of America.* Concord, N.H.: Republican Press Association, 1896.

Williams, D. H. "Stab Wound of Heart and Pericardium—Suture of the Pericardium—Recovery—Patient Alive Three Years Afterward." *Medical Record of New York*, vol. 51 (March 27, 1897).

Who's Who in America, vol. 11, 1920–1921.

Who's Who in American Medicine, New York, 1925.

Who's Who of the Colored Race, vol. 1, 1915.

Baker, Henry E. "The Negro in the Field of Invention." *Journal of Negro History* (March 1913).

Balch, S. W. "Granville T. Woods." *Cosmopolitan Magazine* (April 1895).

Culp, D. W., ed. *Twentieth Century Negro Literature*. Atlanta, Ga.: J. L. Nichols, 1902. (Chapter by Henry Baker, "The Negro as an Inventor.")

Dabney, W. P. *Cincinnati's Colored Citizens*. Cincinnati: Dabney Publishing Co., 1926.

LOUIS T. WRIGHT

Cobb, W. Montague. "Louis Tompkins Wright 1891–1952." *Negro History Bulletin* (May 1953).

Harlem Hospital Clinical Society. "In Memoriam Dr. Louis T. Wright." *Hospital Bulletin*, vol. 6, no. 2 (September 1953).

Ovington, Mary W. *Portraits in Color*. New York: Viking Press, 1927.

Rothman, Michael. Interview of Dr. Wright. WPA Project. Negroes of New York (July 26, 1939).

Scudder, Charles, ed. *Treatment of Fractures*. W. B. Saunders, 1938. (Chapter by Wright, "Head Injuries.")

Wilkins, Roy. "Louis T. Wright: Fighter for Equality and Excellence." *The Crisis*, vol. 7, no. 5 (May 1963).

Wright, L. T. "Factors Controlling Negro Health." *The Crisis*, vol. 42, no. 9 (September 1935).

Wright, L. T. "Aureomycin: A New Antibiotic with Virucidal Properties." *Journal of the American Medical Association*, vol. 38, no. 5 (October 9, 1948).

Wright, L. T., and Wright, Jane. "Further Observations on the Use of Triethylene Melamine in Neoplastic Diseases." *Archives of Internal Medicine* (March 1952).

GENERAL REFERENCES

Cobb, W. Montague. "A New Dawn in Medicine." *Ebony* (September 1963).

Davis, John P., ed. *The American Negro Reference Book*. Englewood Cliffs, N.J.: Prentice Hall, 1966.

Ferguson, Lloyd N. "Negroes in Chemistry." *Industrial Trends*, vol. 6, no. 2 (1949).

Haber, Louis. *The Role of the American Negro in the Fields of Science*. Unpublished manuscript. 1966. Division of Elementary and Secondary Education, Bureau of Research, Office of Education, Washington, D.C. 20202. Project No. 6-8353, ERIC Document 013275.

Hughes, Langston. *Famous American Negroes*. New York: Dodd, Mead, 1961.

Marcus, Lloyd. *The Treatment of Minorities in Secondary School Textbooks*. New York: Anti-Defamation League, 1961.

Roy, J. H. "Contributions of Negro Scientists." *The Crisis*, vol. 46, no. 6 (June 1939).

Staupers, Mabel K. *No Time for Prejudice*. New York: Macmillan, 1961.

Woodson, Carter, and Wesley, C. H. *The Negro in Our History*. 10th edition, Associated Publishers, 1962.

Woodson, Carter. "Negroes Distinguished in Science." *Negro History Bulletin*, vol. 2 (1938–1939).

Picture Credits

Index

Aero-Foam, 134, 139
air brake, automatic, 69
almanac, Banneker's, 8, 12, 14, 15
American Association for Advancement of Science, 158
American Bell Telephone Company, 70
American Board of Surgery, 209, 240
American College of Surgeons, 199, 209, 215
American Engineering Company, 70
American Institute of Chemists, 142, 158
American Medical Association, 196, 213
American Red Cross, 236, 237, 238
Amherst College, 221, 222, 241
anesthesia, 181

Anola, 6
antioxidants, 155–56
antiseptics, 181
arson attempt on Julian's home, 138
arthritis, 137
Aureomycin, 210

bacon, curing of, 156
bacteriology, 180
bandages, sterilization of, 154
Banneker, Benjamin
    family background, 1–3
    first clock built, 5–6
    almanacs, 8, 12, 14, 15
    letter to Jefferson, 8–11
    lays out Washington, D.C., 15–16
    Department of Peace, 16–18
    death, 19
Beattie, John, 223, 224, 234–35

Bell, Alexander Graham, 75
Birth of a Nation, 204
Black Edison, 60
Blanchard, Dean, 125–27, 131
blood banks, 229, 236–38
Blood for Britain project, 234
blood groups, 223
blood plasma, 227–31
blood preservation, 227–28
blood transfusion, 223–24, 226, 227, 229
Blood Transfusion Association, 234–35
bombing attempt on Julian's home, 139–40
Boston Lying-In Hospital, 203–204
Browne, Charles A., 33
Bunche, Ralph, 215

Call and Post, 101
cancer research, 210, 215
Carrel, Alexis, 231
Carver Art Collection, 120
Carver, George Washington
    born a slave, 106
    early schooling, 106
    college training, 106–109
    work on fungus diseases, 109
    and Booker T. Washington, 109–10
    rotation of crops, 111
    peanuts, 111–12
    testimony before
        Congressional Committee, 113–15

Spingarn Medal, 115
    patents, 119
    death, 119–20
Carver Museum, 119–20
Chicago Department of Health Laboratories, 149
Chicago Medical School, 179–80
Chicago, University of, 149, 164, 170
Chicagoan of the Year, 137, 142
Clark University, 203
Cleveland Call, 101
Cleveland Water Works, 95–96
Cobb, W. Montague, 201, 243
Columbia-Presbyterian Medical Center, 226
Condorcet, Marquis de, 12, 19
Congressional committee on tariffs, 113–15
Cornish, James, 186–87
cortexolone, 137
cortisone, 137
Crisis, The, 213–14
crop rotation, 111
cross matching of blood, 224
cytoplasm, 173

Damon Runyon Fund, 210
Dartmouth College, 163
DePauw University, 124, 128
Deutsch, Albert, 237, 242
Douglass, Frederick, 71, 186, 189
Drew, Charles Richard
    background, 219–21

early schooling, 221
athletic ability, 222–23
Amherst College, 222
Morgan State College, 222–23
McGill Medical School, 223–25
Howard Medical School, 223, 225
Freedmen's Hospital, 225–26
Columbia-Presbyterian Medical Center, 226
blood bank work, 227–29, 236
Springarn Medal, 240
honors and awards, 240
death, 241
tributes, 242–44
Du Bois, W. E. B., 197, 217
Dunbar, Paul L., 194
dyes from clays, 113

ectoplasm, 167, 168, 169, 173–74
Edison Electric Light Company, 80–81
Edison Pioneers, 83, 84
Edison, Thomas A., 80, 81, 83, 116
electric railway, 68
electro-mechanical brake, 69
Ellicott, Andrew, 6–7
Ellicott, George, 19
Emancipation Centennial, 102
ether, 181
ethylene oxide gas for sterilization, 153–54

evaporation, multiple, 25–27

Fantus, Bernard, 229
fertilization, 169
flash drying, 151–52
food sterilization, 152–54
Ford, Henry, 116
Franklin, Benjamin, 8
Freedmen's Bureau, 189
Freedmen's Hospital, 188–93, 205, 225–26, 240

Garrison, William Lloyd, 71
gas mask, 88, 91–92
gene theory of inheritance, 168
General Electric Company, 70
George Washington Carver Day, 121
George Washington Carver Foundation, 119
germ theory of disease, 180
glaucoma eye disease, 129
Glidden Company, 133–34
Gresham, Walter, 189
Griffith, Carroll, 148–49
Griffith Laboratories, 149, 150, 159

Hall, George, 185, 196–97, 198
Hall, Lloyd A.
background, 146–48
early education, 148
Northwestern University, 148–49
graduate work, 149
work as a chemist, 149
Griffith Laboratories, 150

Hall, Lloyd A. (*cont.*)
  curing salts, 150
  sterilization of foods and
    spices, 152–53
  antioxidants and rancidity,
    154–56
  protein hydrolysates, 156
  patents, 157
  science adviser in two wars,
    157
  honors, awards, fellowships,
    158–59
Hammer Collection, 81
Hammer, Edwin W., 81
Harlem Hospital, 207–8,
  210–11, 215–16
Harvard Medical School, 203–4
Hawley-Smoot Tariff Bill, 115
Heinrich, Peter, 4
Howard University, 127, 128,
  163, 164, 165, 189, 200,
  223, 225, 226, 234, 240
Howe, Elias, 36

Idlewild, 199–200
Incandescent Electric Lighting,
  82
incubator, egg, 69
Institute of Food Technologists,
  146
International College of
  Surgeons, 211
Iowa Agricultural College, 108

Jamaica train, 23

Jefferson, Thomas, 1, 9–12
  letter to Banneker, 11–12
Johnson, Alice, 194, 199
Julian, Percy L.
  background, 122
  early schooling, 123–24
  DePauw University, 124
  Fisk University, 127
  Howard University, 128
  doctoral work in Vienna, 128
  synthesis of physostigmine,
    129–32
  Glidden Company, 133–36
  arson attempt on home,
    138–39
  bombing attempt on home,
    140
  Julian Laboratories, 141–42
  awards, 141–42
  civil rights activities, 143
  and E. E. Just, 171–72
Just, Ernest Everett
  early background, 161
  early schooling, 161
  Dartmouth College, 163
  Howard University, 163
  Marine Biological
    Laboratories, Woods Hole,
    Mass., 164, 166
  University of Chicago, 164,
    170
  gene theory opposed, 168,
    173
  work in foreign laboratories,
    171

publications, 172–73
death, 174

Kaiser Wilhelm Institute for
Biology, 171
King, Martin Luther, 143

Landsteiner, Karl, 223, 231
lasting machine, 40–46
Latimer, Lewis H.
background, 71–73
Civil War service, 73
office boy and draftsman, 60
marriage, 74
work with Alexander Graham
Bell, 75
first invention, 75
work with Hiram Maxim,
75–76
invention of lamp filament, 77
installed electric light plants,
78
association with Thomas
Edison, 80–81
Edison Pioneers, 83, 84
dedication of school to
Latimer, 86
L'Ecole Centrale, 21
legumes, 111
L'Enfant, Pierre Charles, 15
Levi, Josef, 5
Liberator, The, 72
Lillie, Frank, 164, 166, 170,
174
Lister, Sir Joseph, 180, 181
Loeb, Jacques, 172

lubricating cup, 55
lubrication, 53–55
lymphogranuloma venereum, 210

Marine Biological Laboratories,
164, 166
Maryland Historical Society, 19
Matzeliger, Jan E.
background, 36
apprenticeship at ten, 37
in Lynn, Mass., 38–39
church participation, 39,
48–49
work on shoe machines,
40–48
lasting machine, 44–46
financial backing, 42–43
death, 48
Maxim, Hiram, 75–76
Mayo, Charles, 183
McCoy, Elijah
background, 51–52
apprenticeship in Scotland, 52
railroad fireman, 53
lubrication inventions, 55–59
father of lubrication, 58
"the real McCoy," 59
McGill Medical School, 223
McLaughry, D. O., 242
military food supplies, 157
Morgan, Garrett A.
background, 88
marriage, 90
hair-straightening invention,
91

Morgan, Garrett A. (*cont.*)
  safety hood, 91–98
  traffic signal, 97, 98–99
  civil rights activities, 101
  blindness and death, 102

Naples Zoological Station, 171
National Archives, 115, 189
National Association for the
  Advancement of Colored
  People, 101, 143, 159, 197,
  200, 214, 240
National Cancer Institute, 210
National Medical Association,
  196, 200
National Safety Device
  Company, 92–94
Negro People's Committee, 214
Nereis (sandworm), 164
New York Academy of
  Medicine, 236
nitrates in soil, 110
North American Committee to
  Aid Spanish Democracy, 214
Northwestern University,
  148–49
nurse training program, 184,
  192–93, 200

Oak Park, Ill., (Julian's home),
  138

Packwood, Theodore, 28–29
Pammell, Louis H., 108–9
parthenogenesis, 165
Pasteur, Louis, 180–81
Peace, Department of, 16–18

peanuts, uses of, 111–12
Penn, William F., 203
pericardium, 187
physostigmine, synthesis of,
  129–32
Pikl, Josef, 129
Pitt, William, 19
plasma, blood, 227–31
Plasma for France project, 232
police surgeon (Wright), 208
polyspermy in marine eggs, 169
preservation of blood, 229, 230
progesterone, 136
protein hydrolysates, 156
Provident Hospital, 185, 186,
  188–89, 192, 198–99
Purvis, Charles B., 189–91,
  193

railway telegraphy, 64
rancidity, 154–55
Reconstruction Period, 191
Rillieux, Norbert
  background, 20–21
  studies in Paris, 21
  sugar refining process, 22–25
  multiple evaporation, 25–29
  "Rillieux System," 29–30
  life in New Orleans for
    Rillieux, 30–31
  plan for draining swamps, 31
  later years in Paris, 31–32
  death, 32
  contributions, 33–34
  commemoration, 34–35
Robbins, Lenore, 229

Robinson, Robert, 130–31
Rockefeller Foundation, 172
Roosevelt, Franklin D., 104
Rosenwald Fund, 130, 212, 225

safety hood, 91–94
St. Luke's Hospital, 199
salts, curing, 150
Schick test, 205
Scudder, Charles, 208
Scudder, John, 226, 230, 232
Simpson College, 107
smallpox vaccination, 206
Smith, Hoke, 189
Smith, Klein & French, 142
Sorbonne, Paris, 171
Southern Christian Leadership
    Conference, 143
soybean, 127, 133–34, 136,
    141
Späth, Ernst, 127
spermatozoa, 165
spices, sterilization of, 152–54
Spingarn Medal, 115, 165, 174,
    209, 240
sterilization of food, 152–54
sterols, 134, 136
Stokes, Carl, 101
Student Nonviolent Coordinating
    Committee, 144
sugar industry, 27
surgical shock, 226–27
sweet potato, 112

tariff, peanut, 113–15

Teachers Union of New York,
    119
telegraphony, 63–64
telephone transmitter, 63
Terramycin, 210
testosterone, 136
third rail, 68
traffic light signal, 97, 98–99
Tuskegee Institute, 109–10,
    116, 119, 214, 229

Union League Club of Chicago,
    141
United Shoe Machinery
    Corporation, 47–48

vacuum pan, 23–28

Wallace, Henry, 114–17
Walsh, Molly, 1
Warfield, William A., 193
Washington, D.C., 1, 15
Washington, Booker T.,
    109–10, 195–97
Ways and Means Committee,
    13–15
Westinghouse Air Brake
    Company, 69
Whitney, Eli, 36
Williams, Daniel Hale
    background, 176–78
    barber in Janesville, 178
    medical apprenticeship, 179
    Chicago Medical School,
        179–180
    Provident Hospital, 185–87

Williams, Daniel Hale (*cont.*)
 "Sewed Up His Heart," 176,
  187–88
 Freedmen's Hospital, 188–93
 nurse training program, 184,
  192, 200
 marriage, 194
 and Booker T. Washington,
  195–97
 death, 199–200
Winslow, Sidney, 47
Woods Electric Company, 66
Woods, Granville T.
 background, 60
 fireman and engineer, 60–61
 telephone transmitter, 62–63
 telegraphony, 63–64
 railway telegraphy, 64
 electric railway, 68
 automatic air brake, 69
 egg incubator, 69
Woods Hole, Mass., 164–66

Wright, Barbara, 215
Wright, Corinne, 207, 209, 217
Wright, Jane, 211, 215
Wright, Louis Tompkins
 background, 201–3
 early schooling, 201–2
 Clark University, 201–2, 203
 Harvard Medical School,
  203–4
 discrimination at Harvard,
  203–4
 picketing *Birth of a Nation*,
  204
 Freedmen's Hospital, 205
 army experience, 206–7
 Harlem Hospital, 207–8
 Spingarn Medal, 209
 antibiotic research, 210
 cancer research, 210–11
 civil rights activities, 211–15
 death, 215

Have you read these ODYSSEY paperbacks?

ODYSSEY CLASSICS

L. M. Boston
THE CHILDREN OF GREEN KNOWE
TREASURE OF GREEN KNOWE
THE RIVER AT GREEN KNOWE
A STRANGER AT GREEN KNOWE
AN ENEMY AT GREEN KNOWE

Edward Eager
HALF MAGIC
KNIGHT'S CASTLE
MAGIC BY THE LAKE
MAGIC OR NOT?
SEVEN-DAY MAGIC
THE TIME GARDEN
THE WELL-WISHERS

Elizabeth Enright
GONE-AWAY LAKE
RETURN TO GONE-AWAY

Eleanor Estes
GINGER PYE
THE WITCH FAMILY

Carolyn Haywood
"B" IS FOR BETSY
BETSY AND BILLY
BACK TO SCHOOL WITH BETSY
BETSY AND THE BOYS

Anne Holm
NORTH TO FREEDOM

Carol Kendall
THE GAMMAGE CUP

Eleanor Frances Lattimore
LITTLE PEAR
LITTLE PEAR AND HIS FRIENDS

Mary Norton
BED-KNOB AND BROOMSTICK
THE BORROWERS
THE BORROWERS AFIELD
THE BORROWERS AFLOAT
THE BORROWERS ALOFT
THE BORROWERS AVENGED

Carl Sandburg
PRAIRIE-TOWN BOY
ROOTABAGA STORIES, PART ONE
ROOTABAGA STORIES, PART TWO

Virginia Sorensen
MIRACLES ON MAPLE HILL

William O. Steele
THE BUFFALO KNIFE
FLAMING ARROWS
THE PERILOUS ROAD
WINTER DANGER

John R. Tunis
THE KID FROM TOMKINSVILLE
WORLD SERIES
KEYSTONE KIDS
ROOKIE OF THE YEAR
YEA! WILDCATS!
A CITY FOR LINCOLN
IRON DUKE
THE DUKE DECIDES
ALL-AMERICAN
CHAMPION'S CHOICE

Henry Winterfeld
CASTAWAY IN LILLIPUT
DETECTIVES IN TOGAS
MYSTERY OF THE ROMAN RANSOM
TROUBLE AT TIMPETILL

Milton Meltzer
UNDERGROUND MAN

Turn the page for more Odyssey titles and ordering information.

ODYSSEY BOOKS

Burke Davis
BLACK HEROES OF THE AMERICAN REVOLUTION

Patricia Harrison Easton
SUMMER'S CHANCE

Louis Haber
BLACK PIONEERS OF SCIENCE AND INVENTION

Lynn Hall
MURDER IN A PIG'S EYE

Virginia Hamilton
A WHITE ROMANCE
JUSTICE AND HER BROTHERS
DUSTLAND
THE GATHERING

Gary Soto
BASEBALL IN APRIL AND OTHER STORIES

Theodore Taylor
AIR RAID—PEARL HARBOR!

Paul Robert Walker
PRIDE OF PUERTO RICO

ODYSSEY/GREAT EPISODES

Kristiana Gregory
JENNY OF THE TETONS
THE LEGEND OF JIMMY SPOON

Len Hilts
QUANAH PARKER

Dorothea Jensen
THE RIDDLE OF PENNCROFT FARM

Seymour Reit
BEHIND REBEL LINES
GUNS FOR GENERAL WASHINGTON

Look for Odyssey paperbacks in your local bookstore.
To order directly from Harcourt Brace, call 1-800-543-1918.